Insects

ISBN 978-1546699460

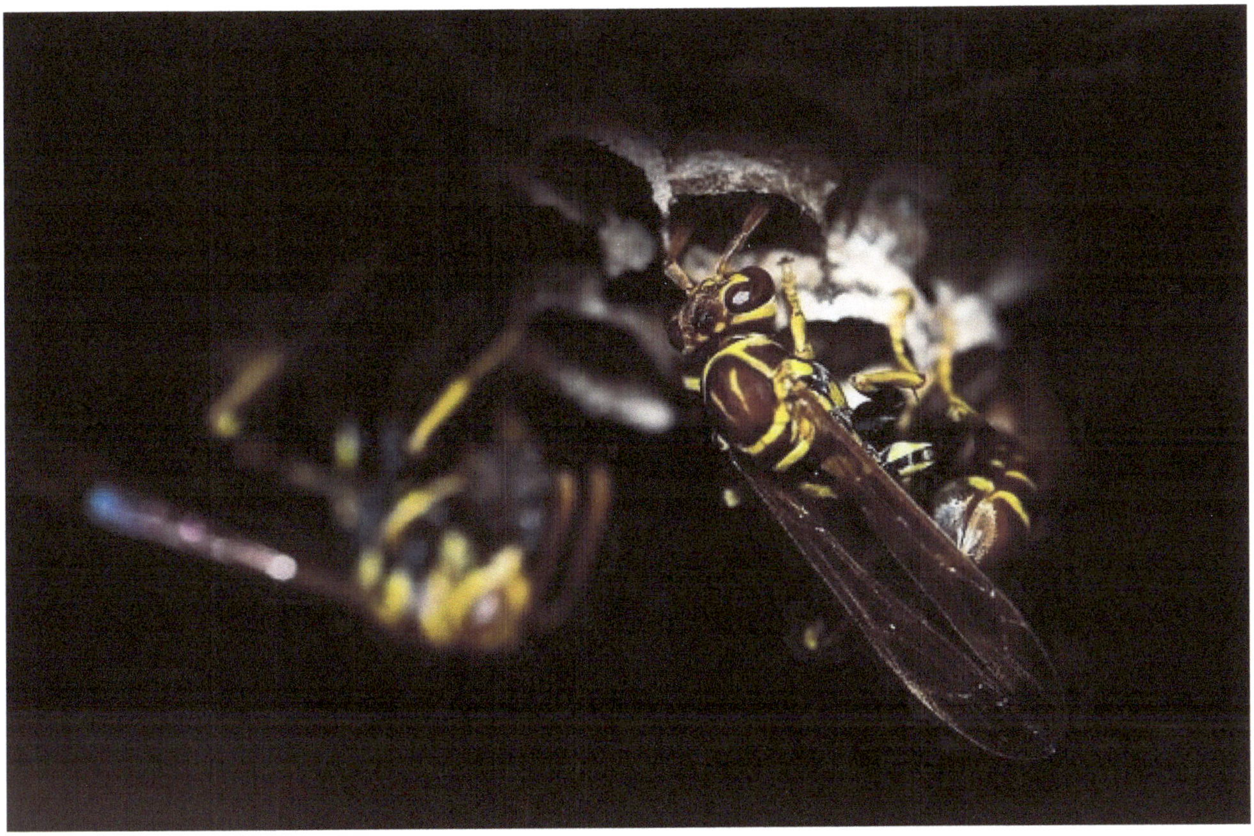

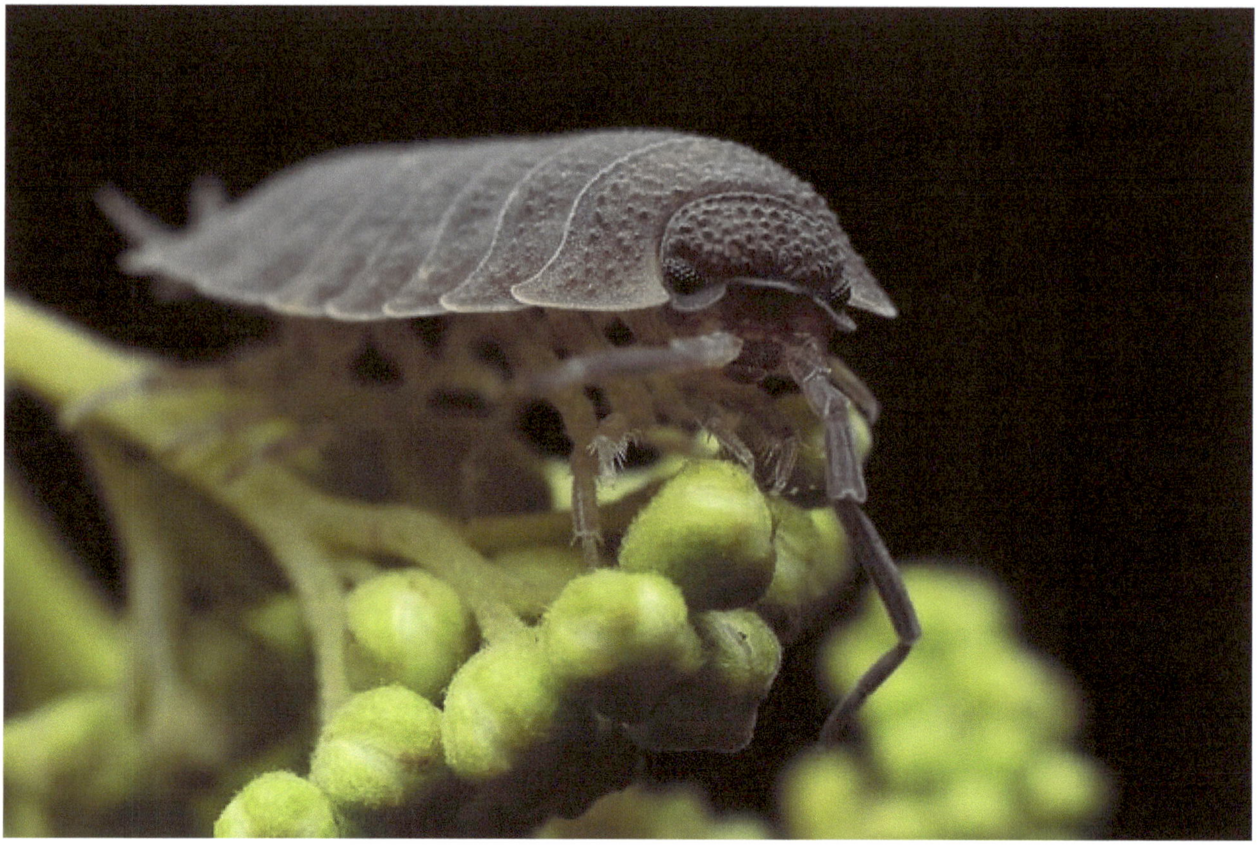

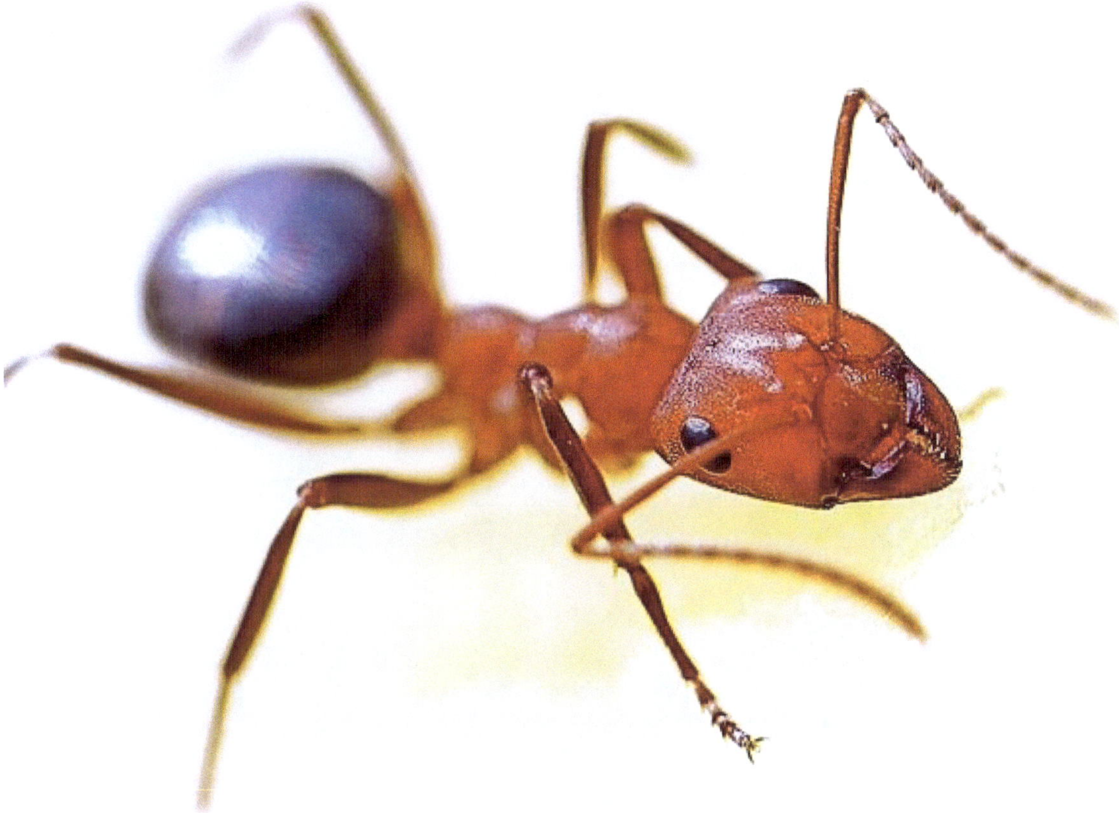

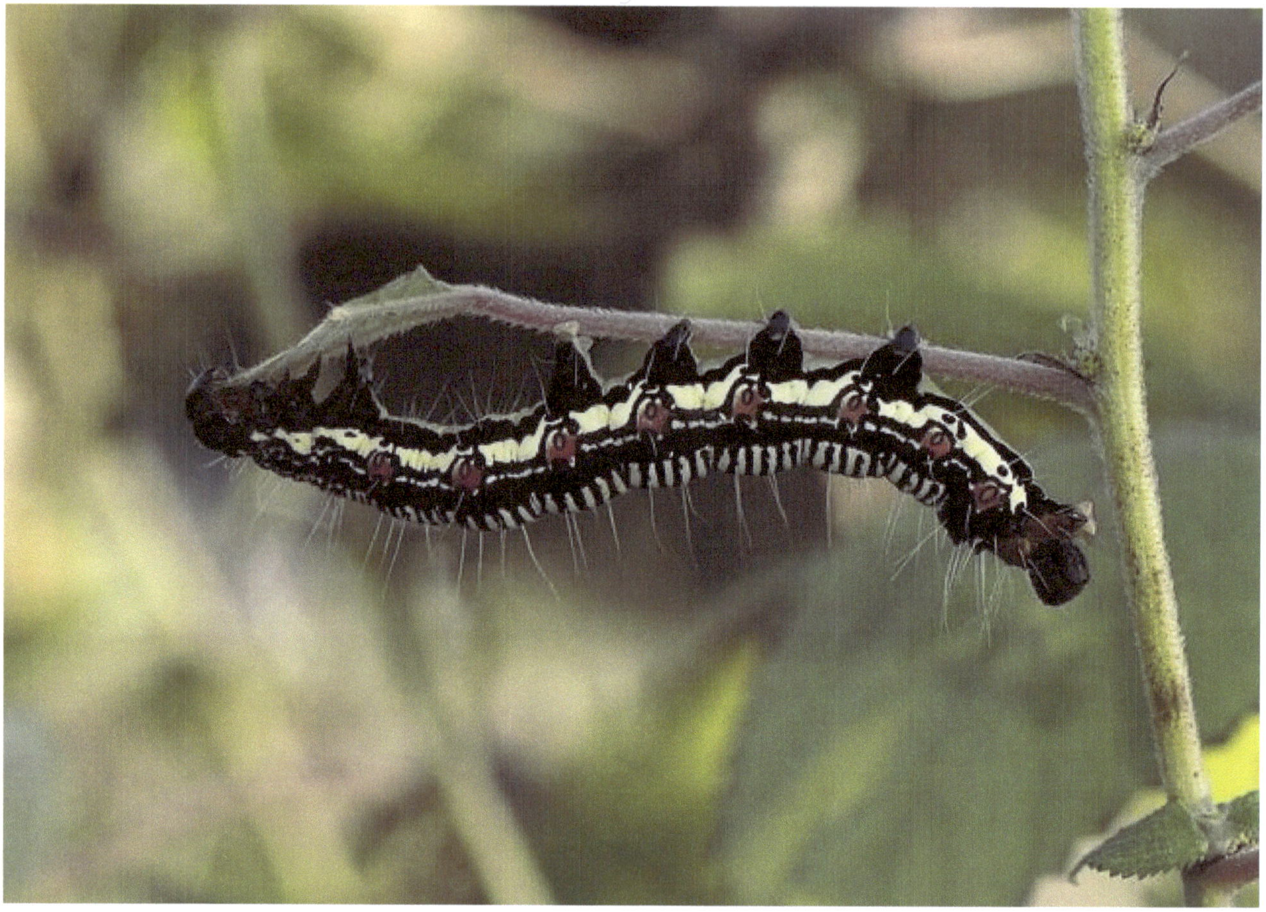

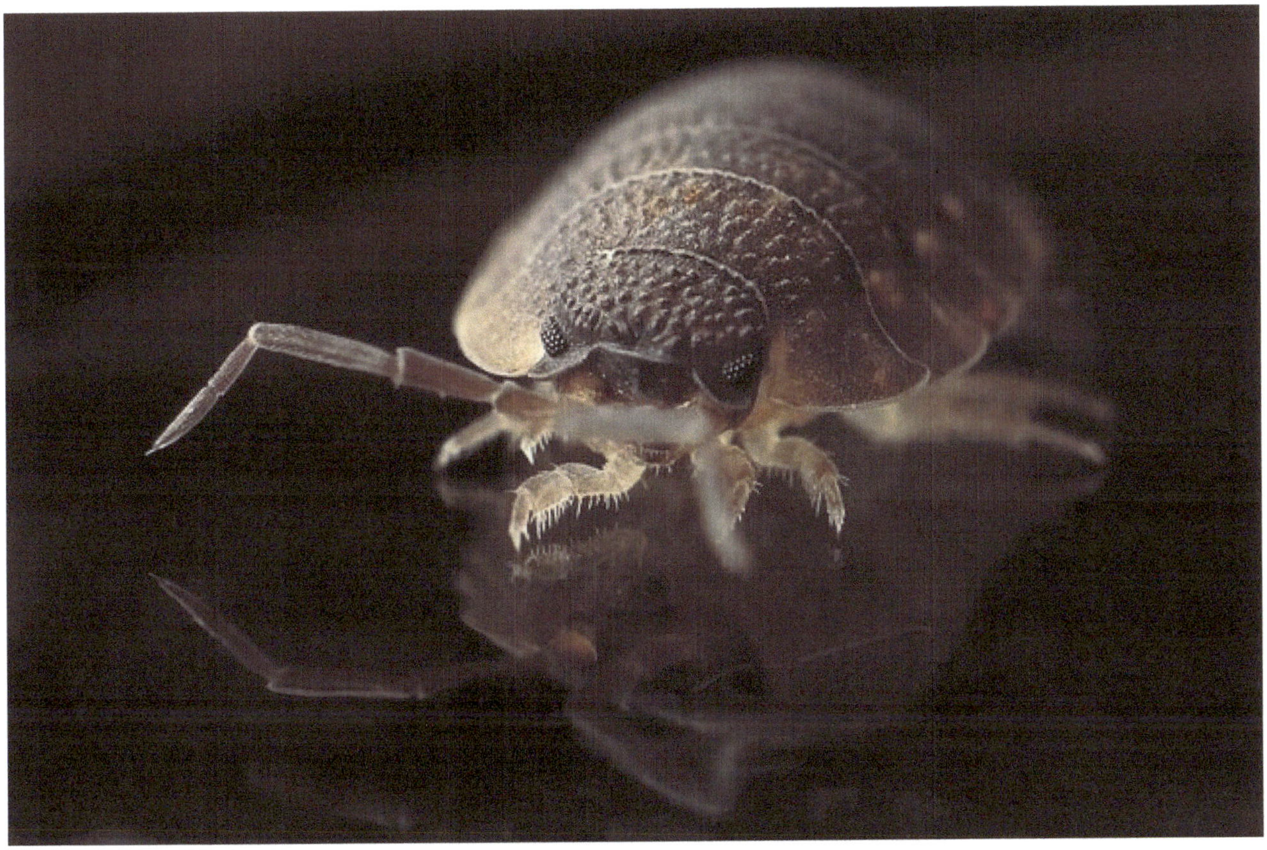

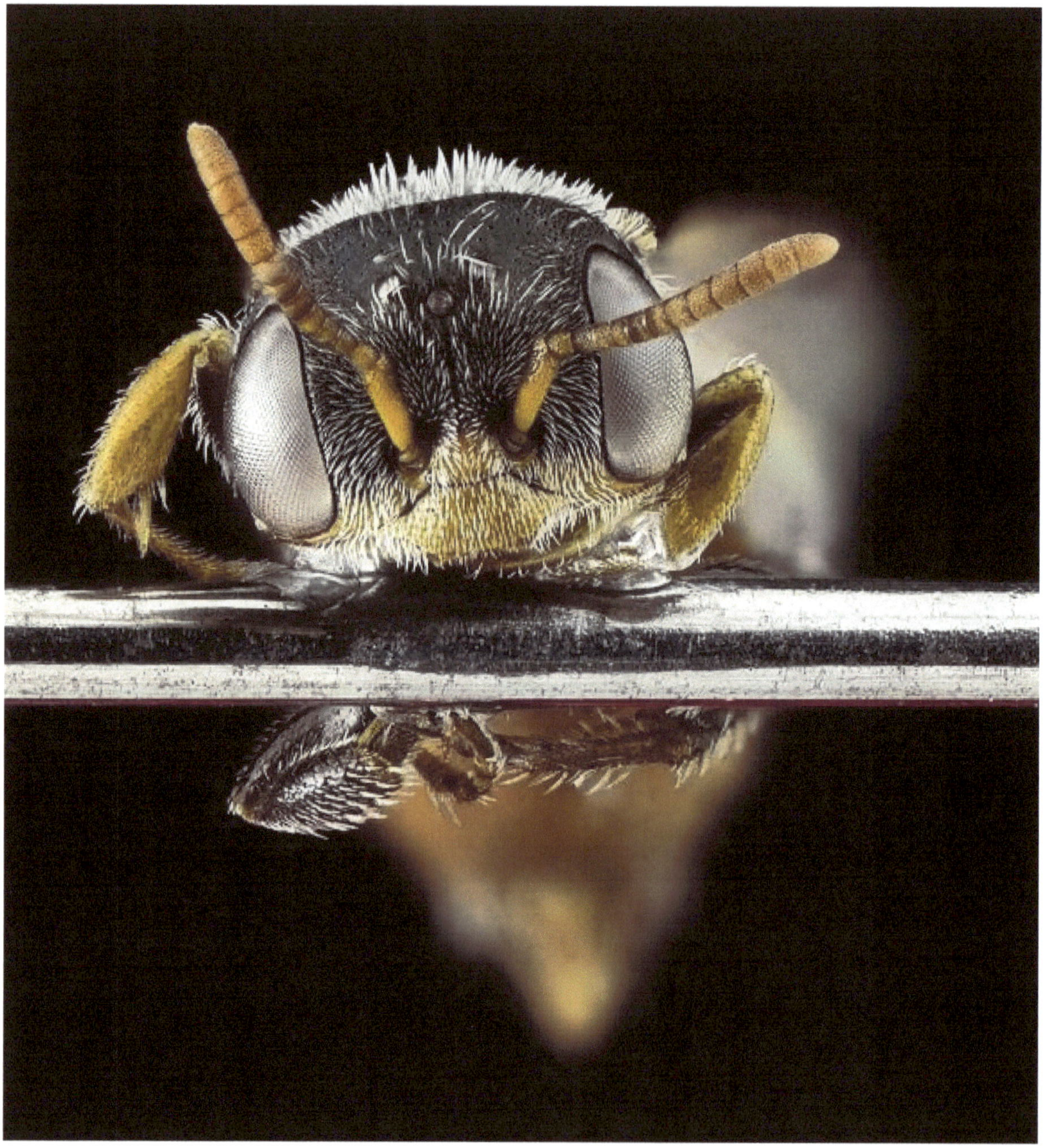

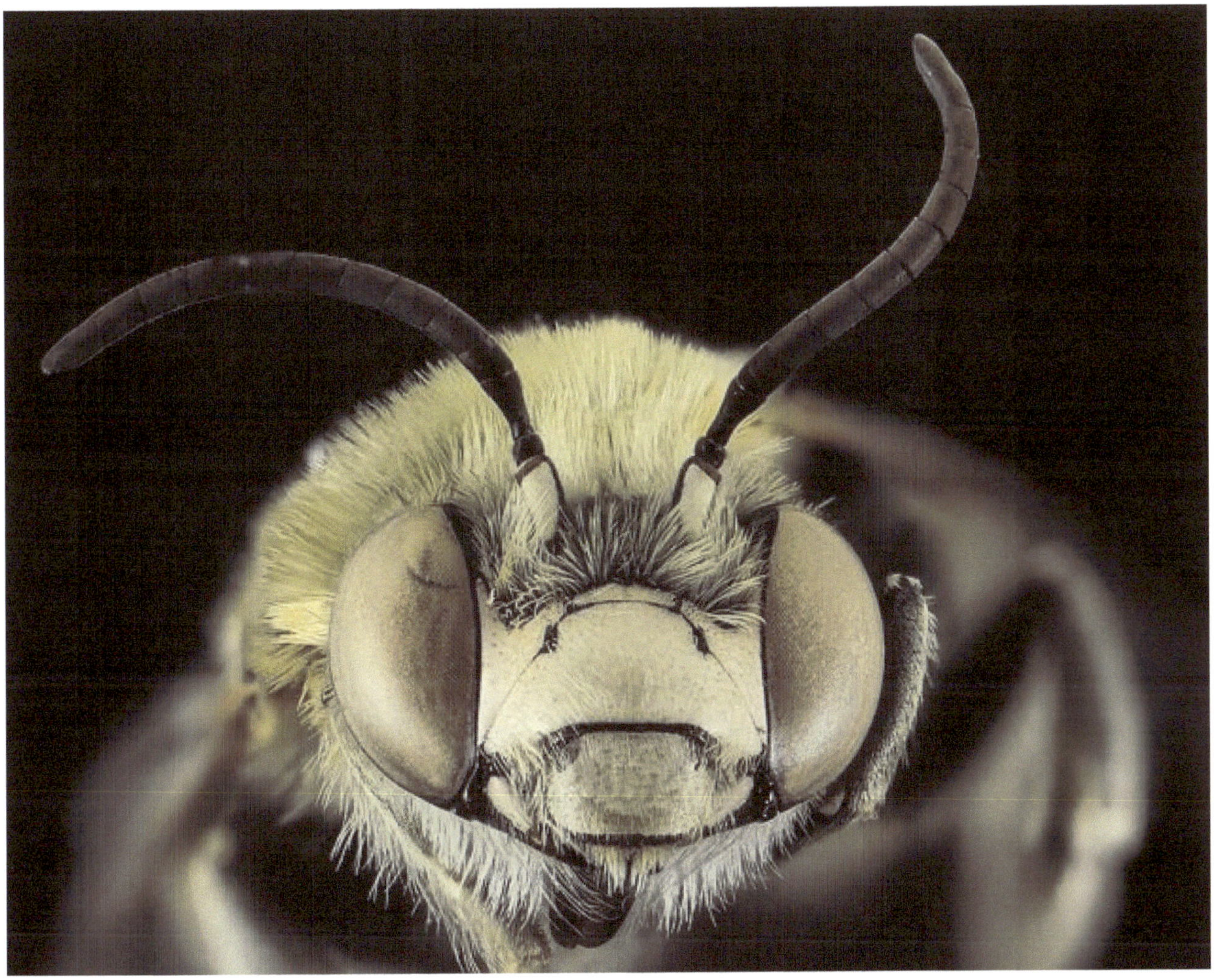

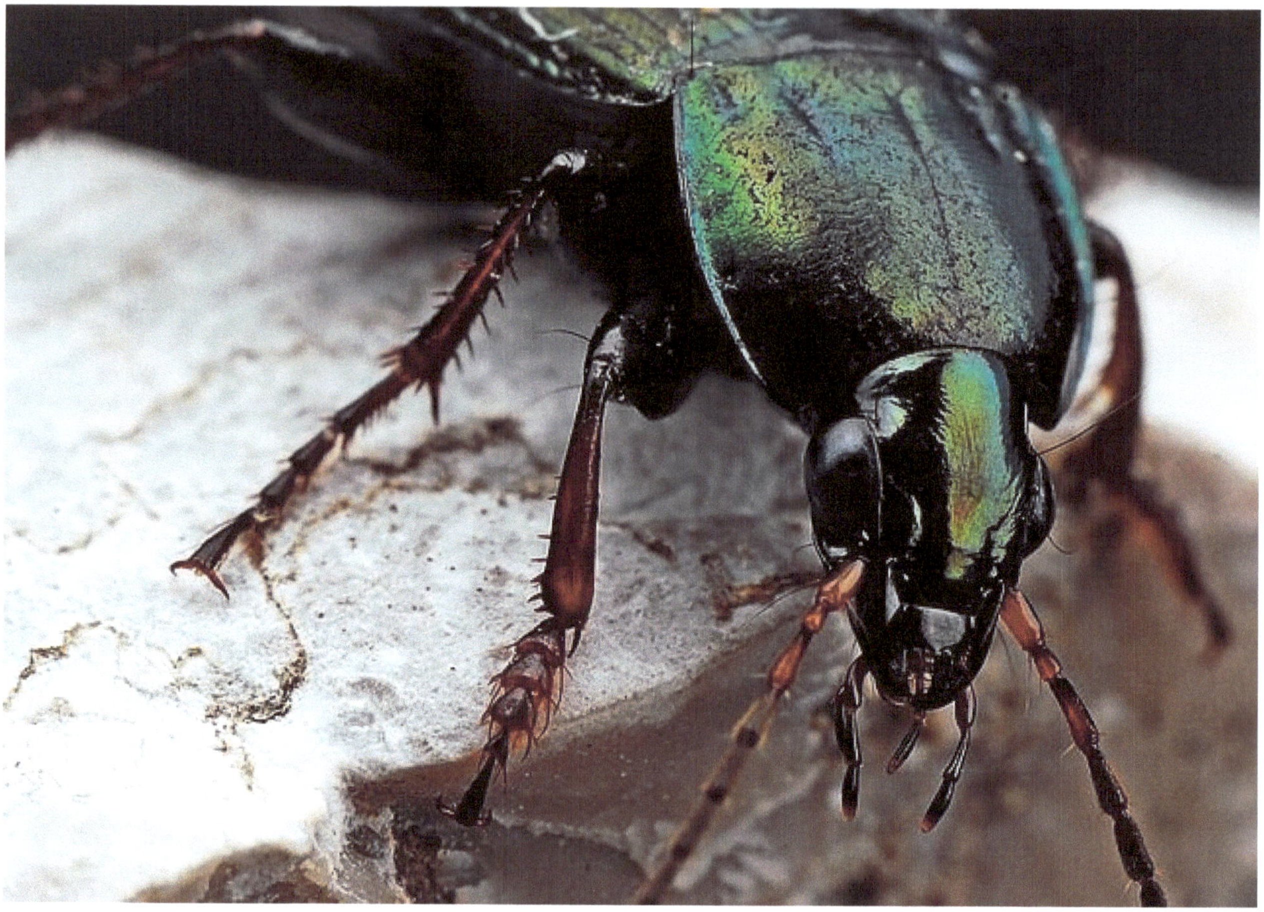

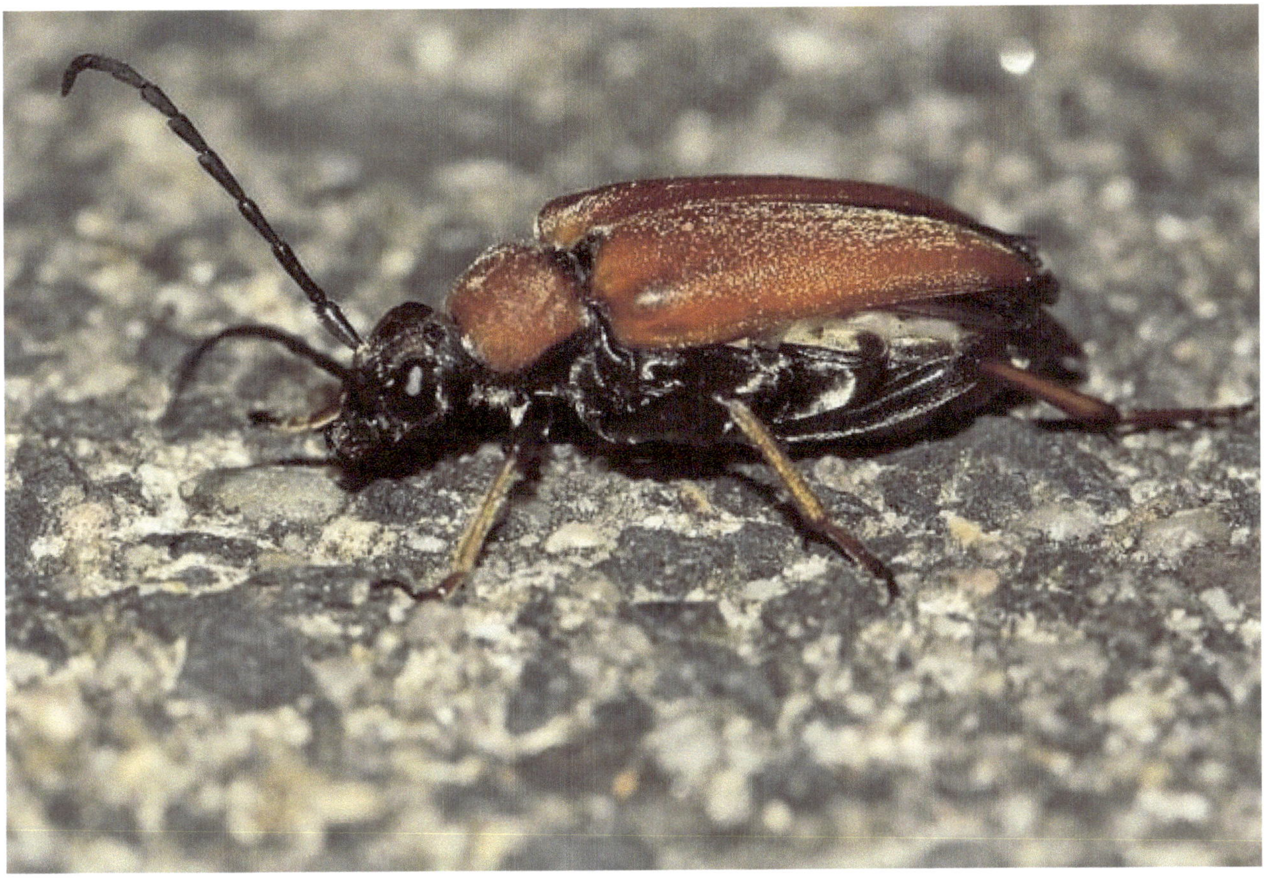

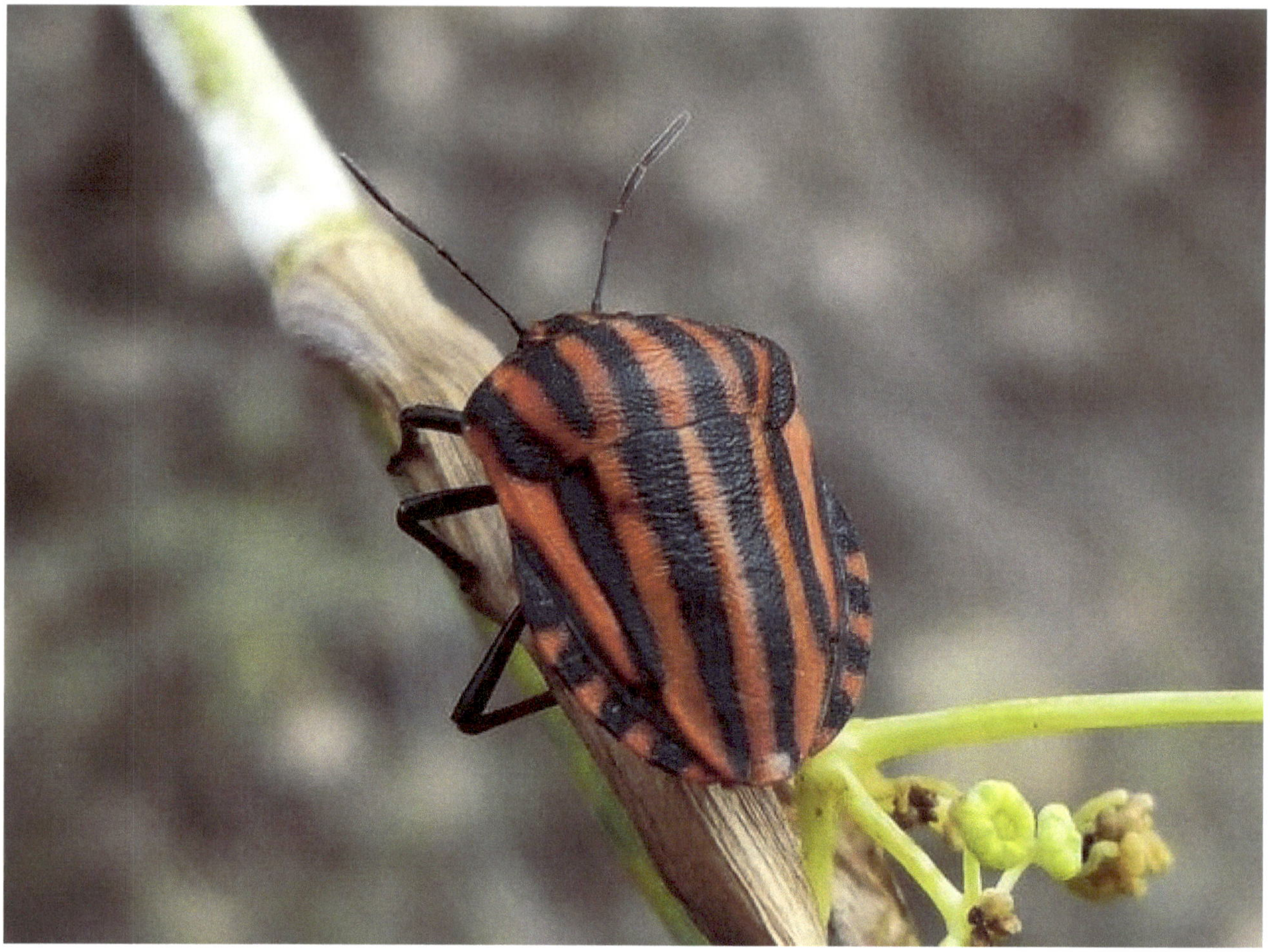

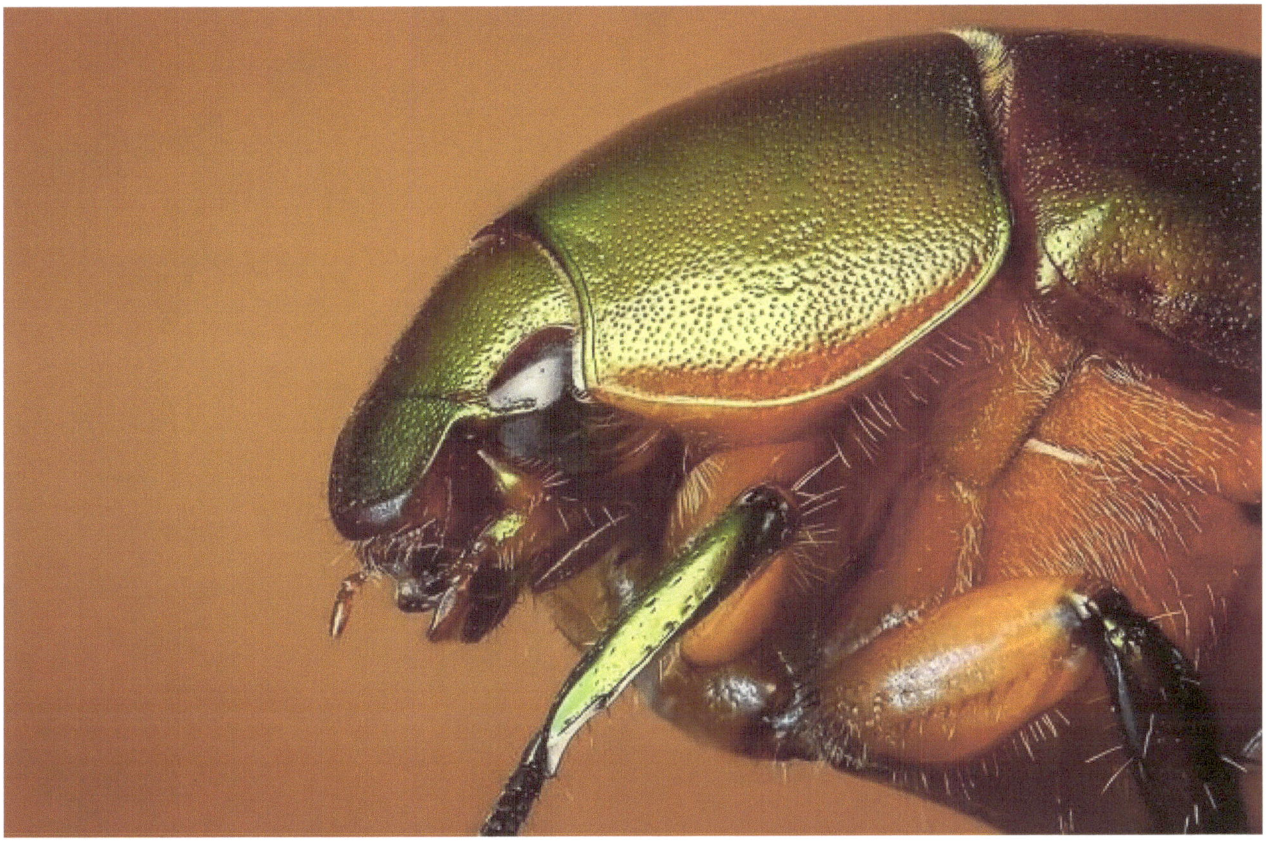

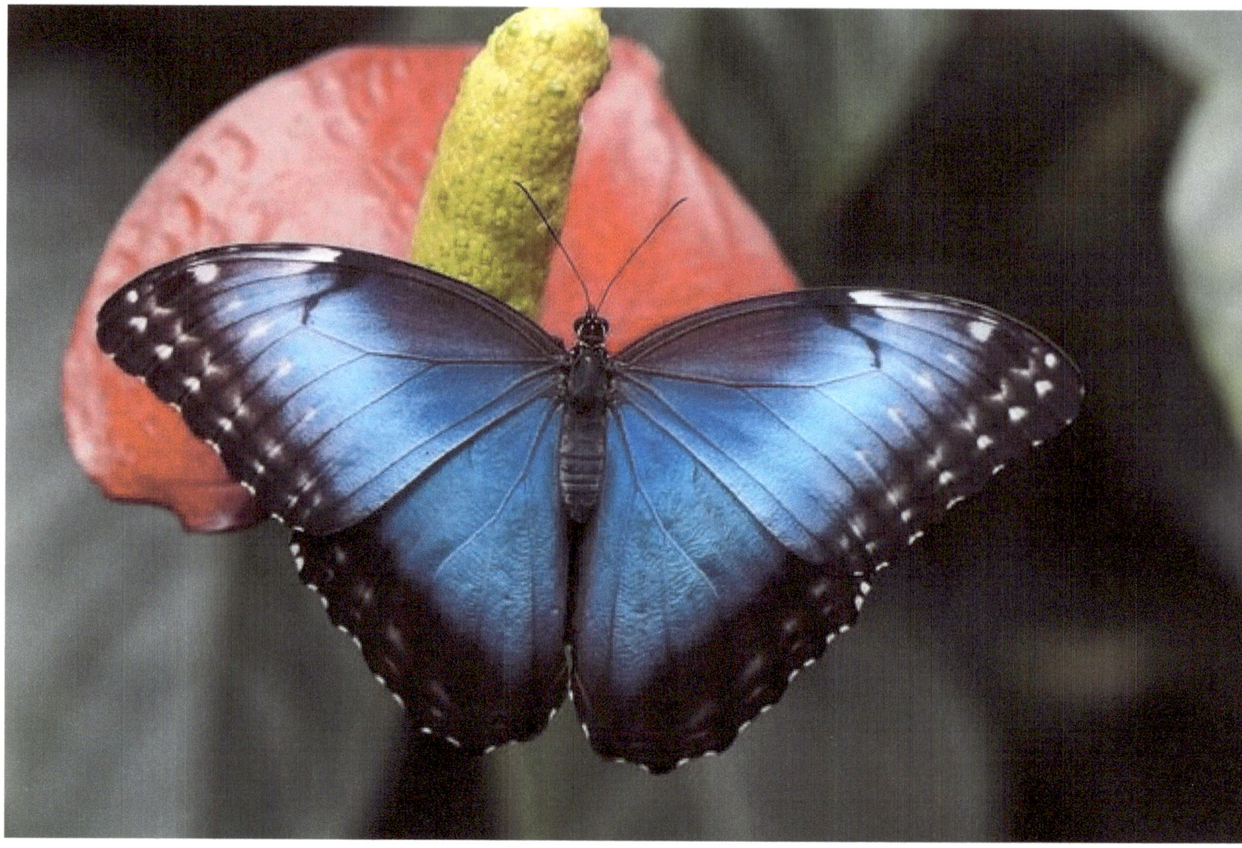

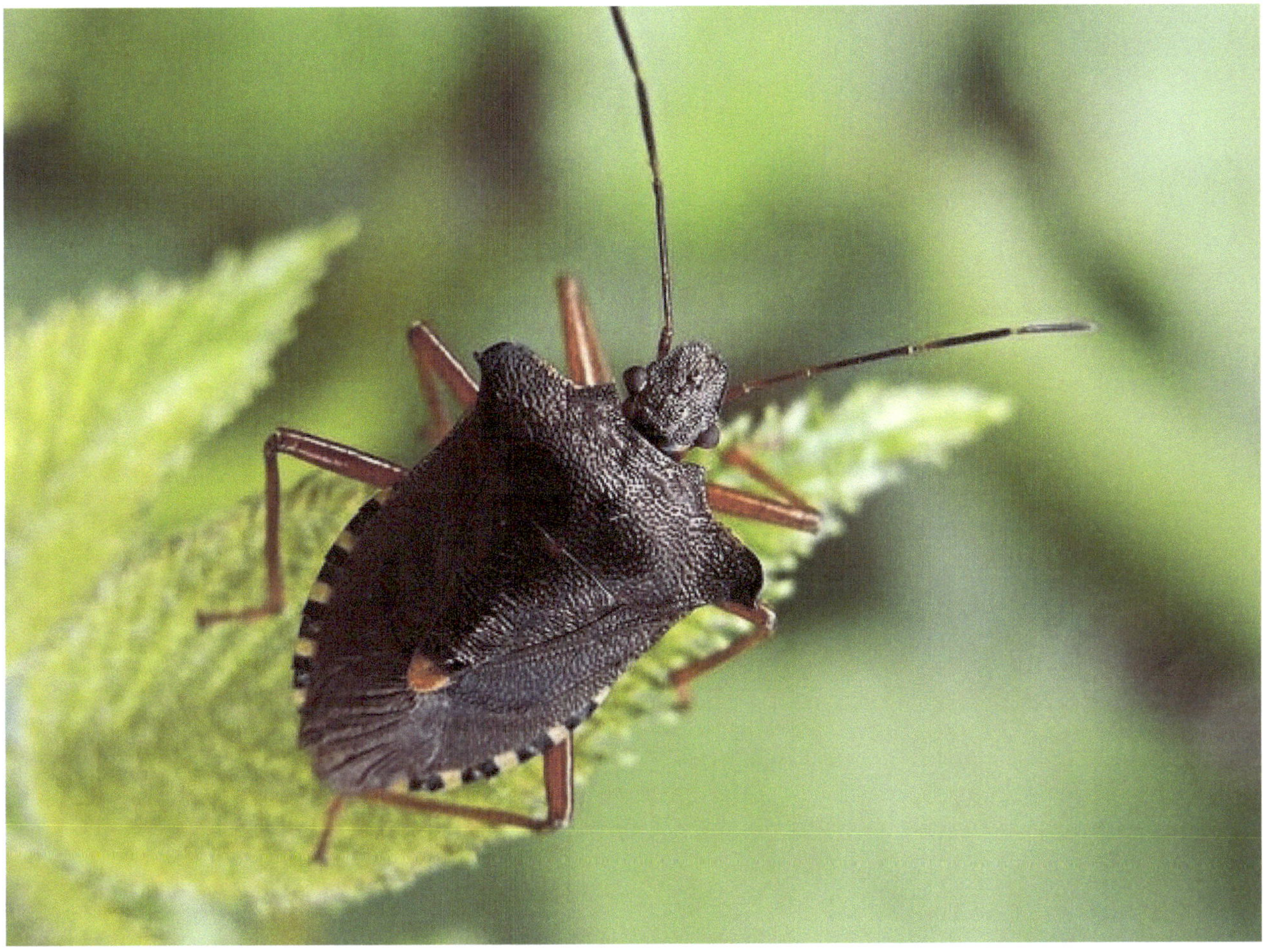

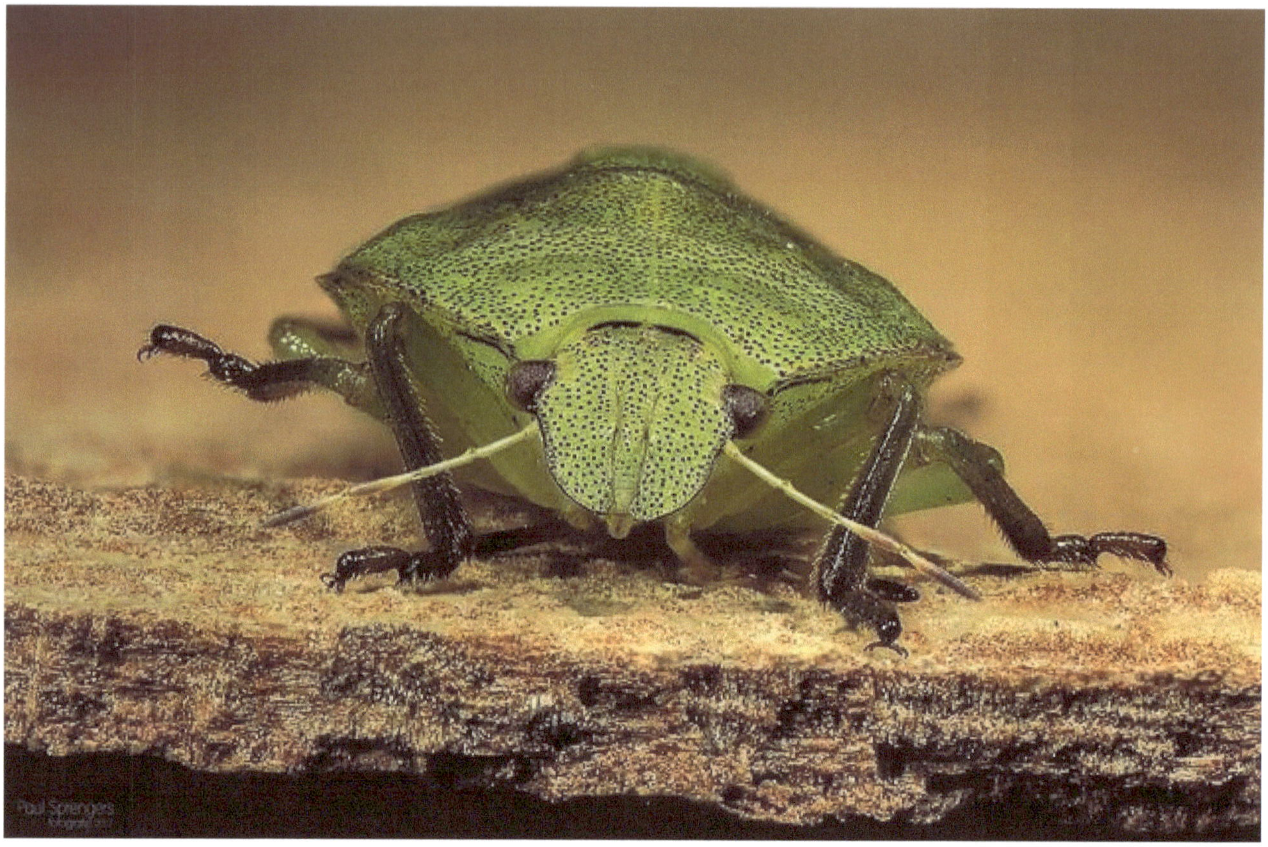
Paul Sprengers

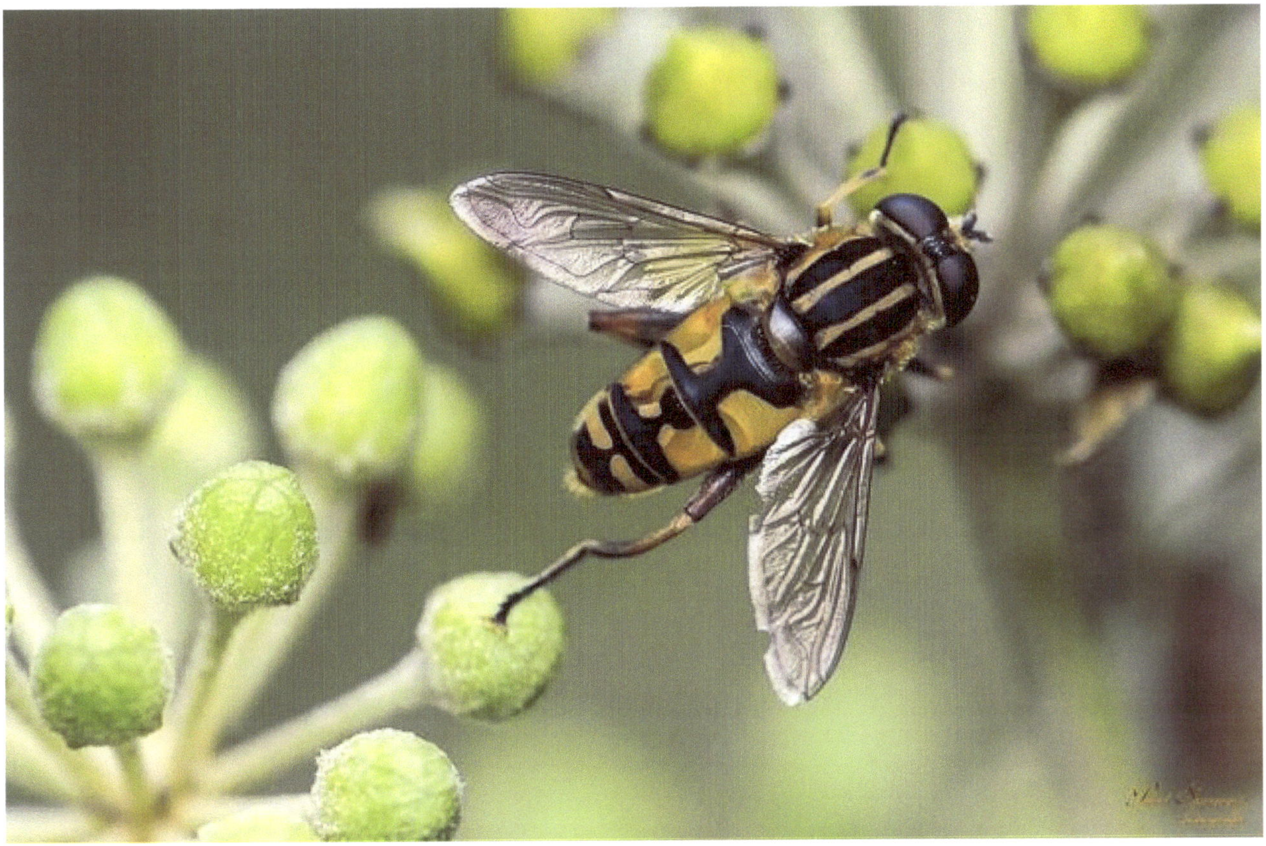

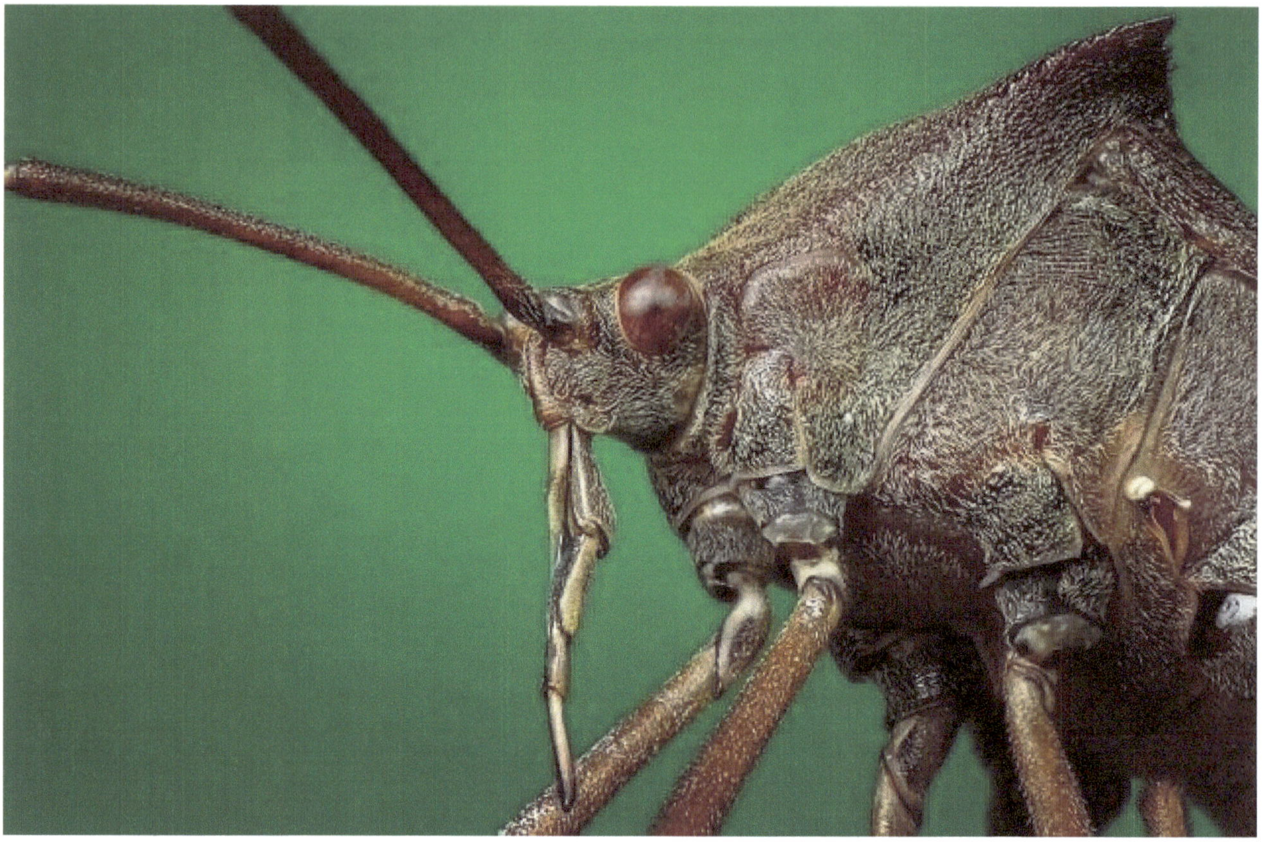

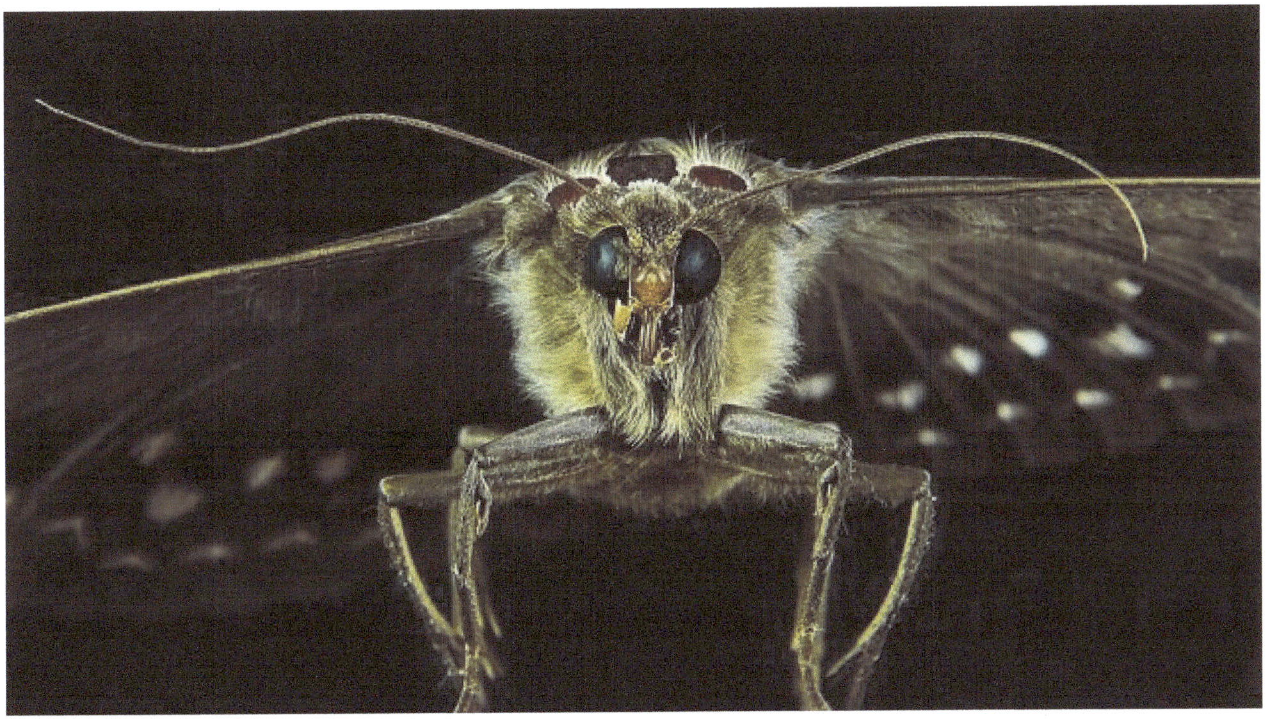

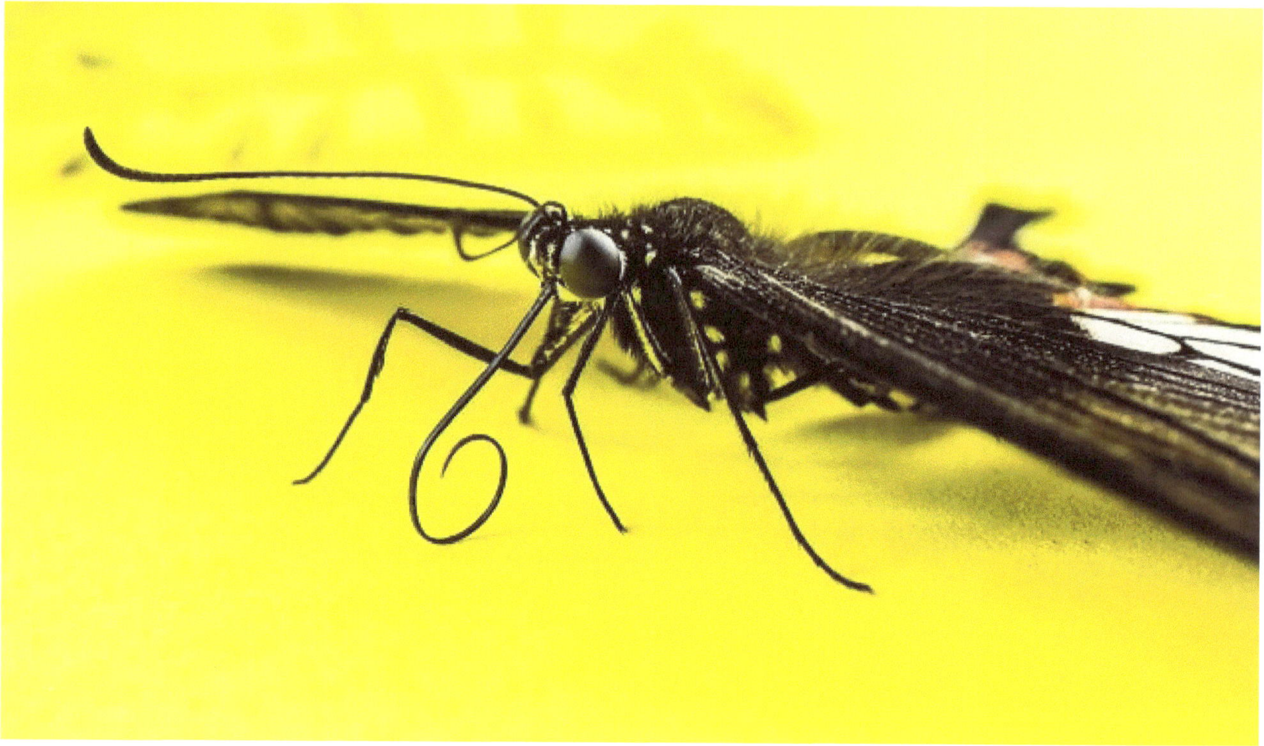

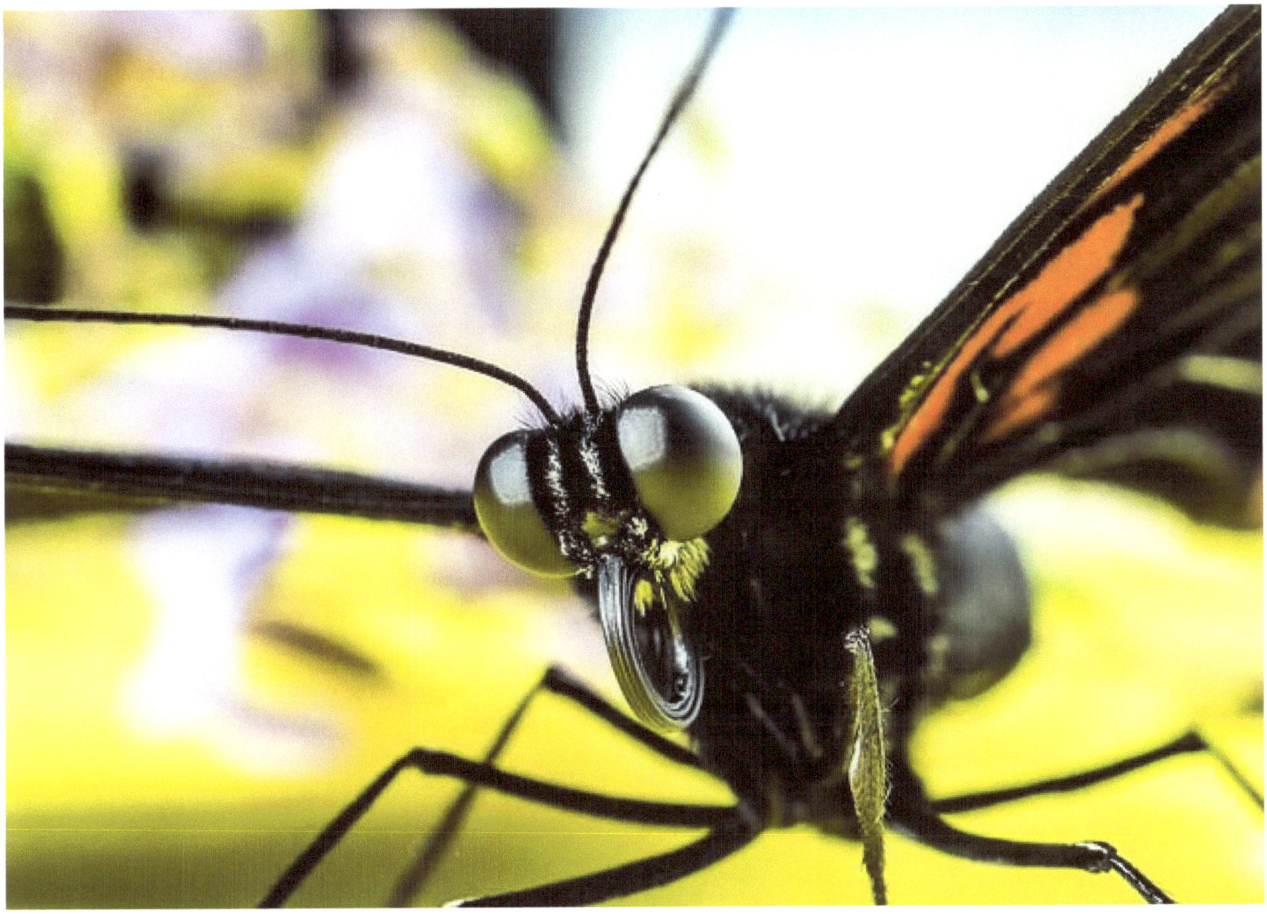

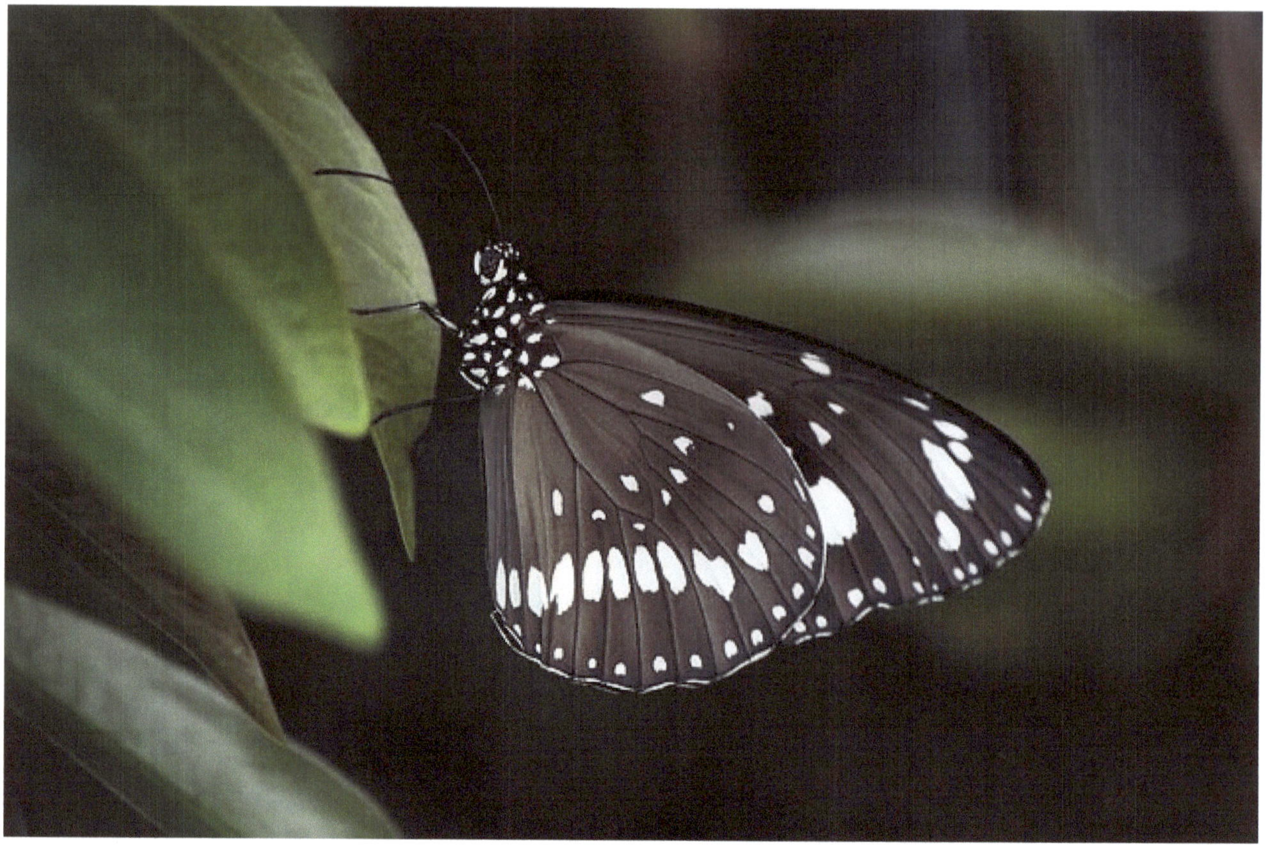

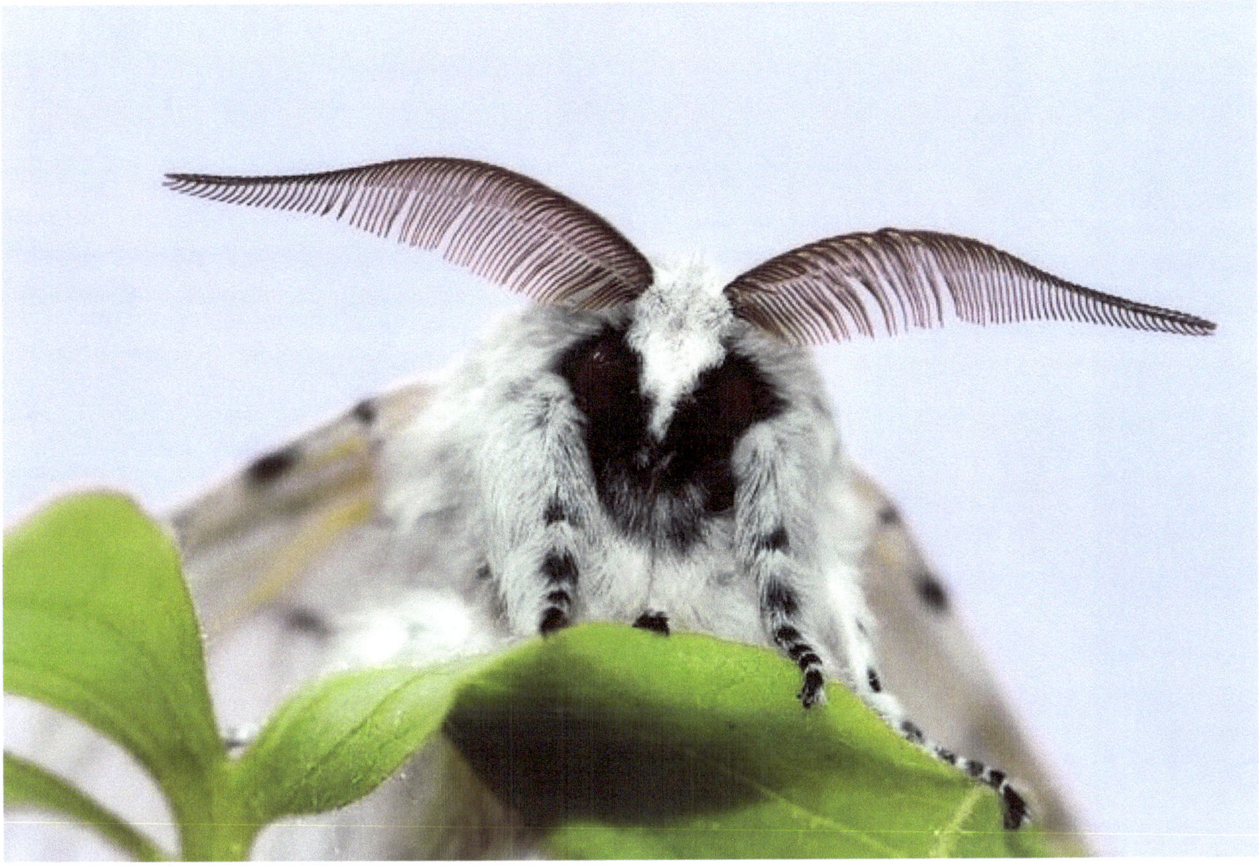

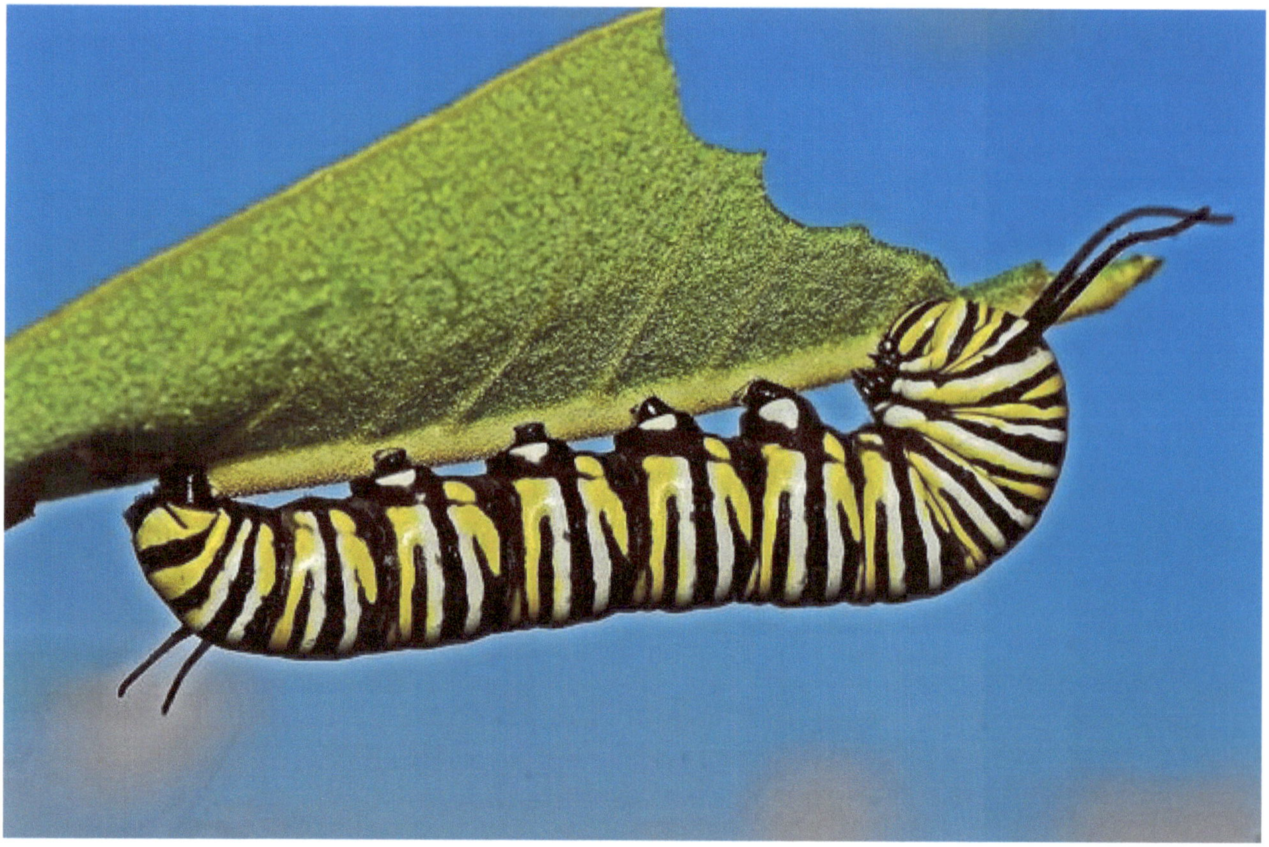

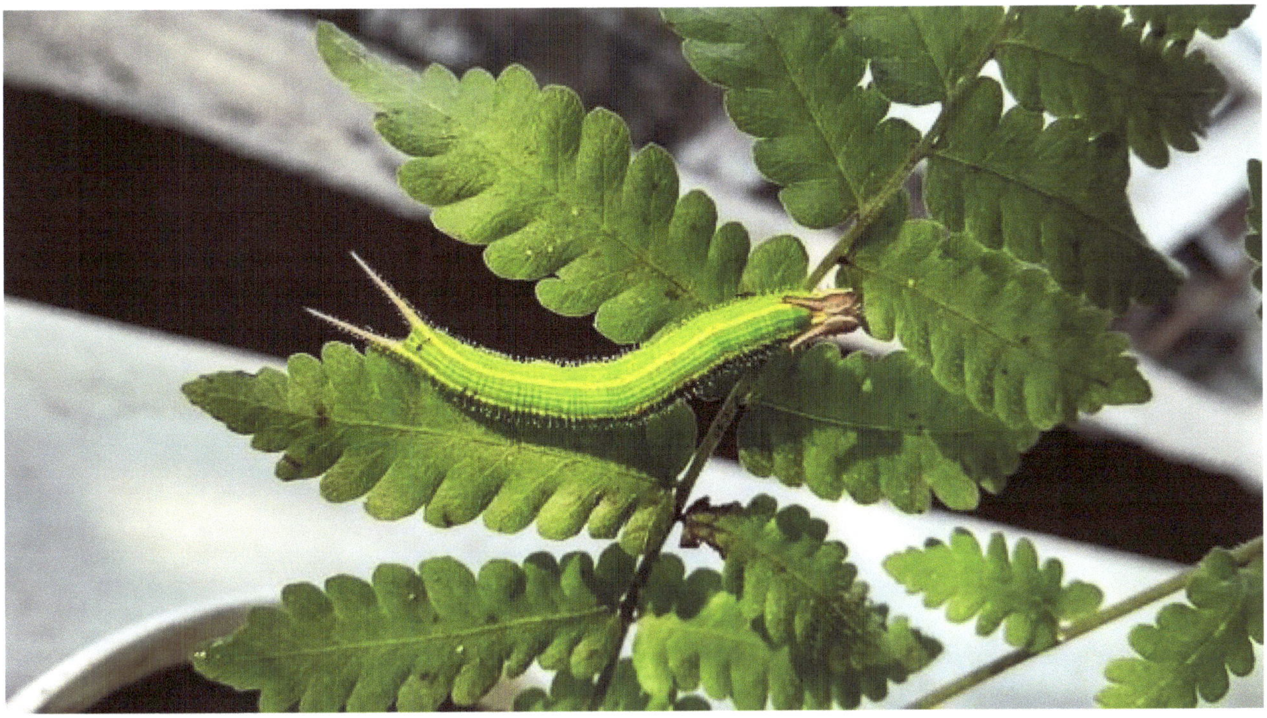

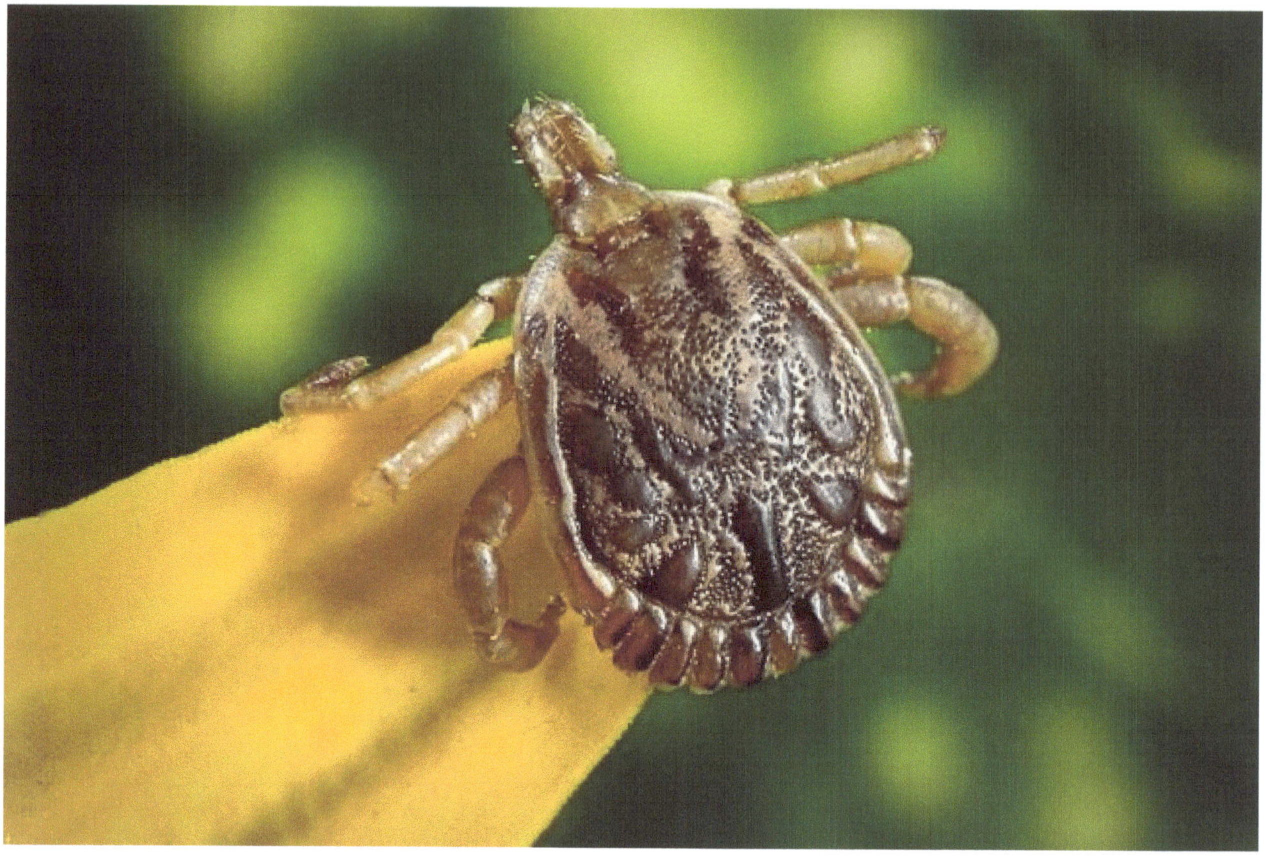

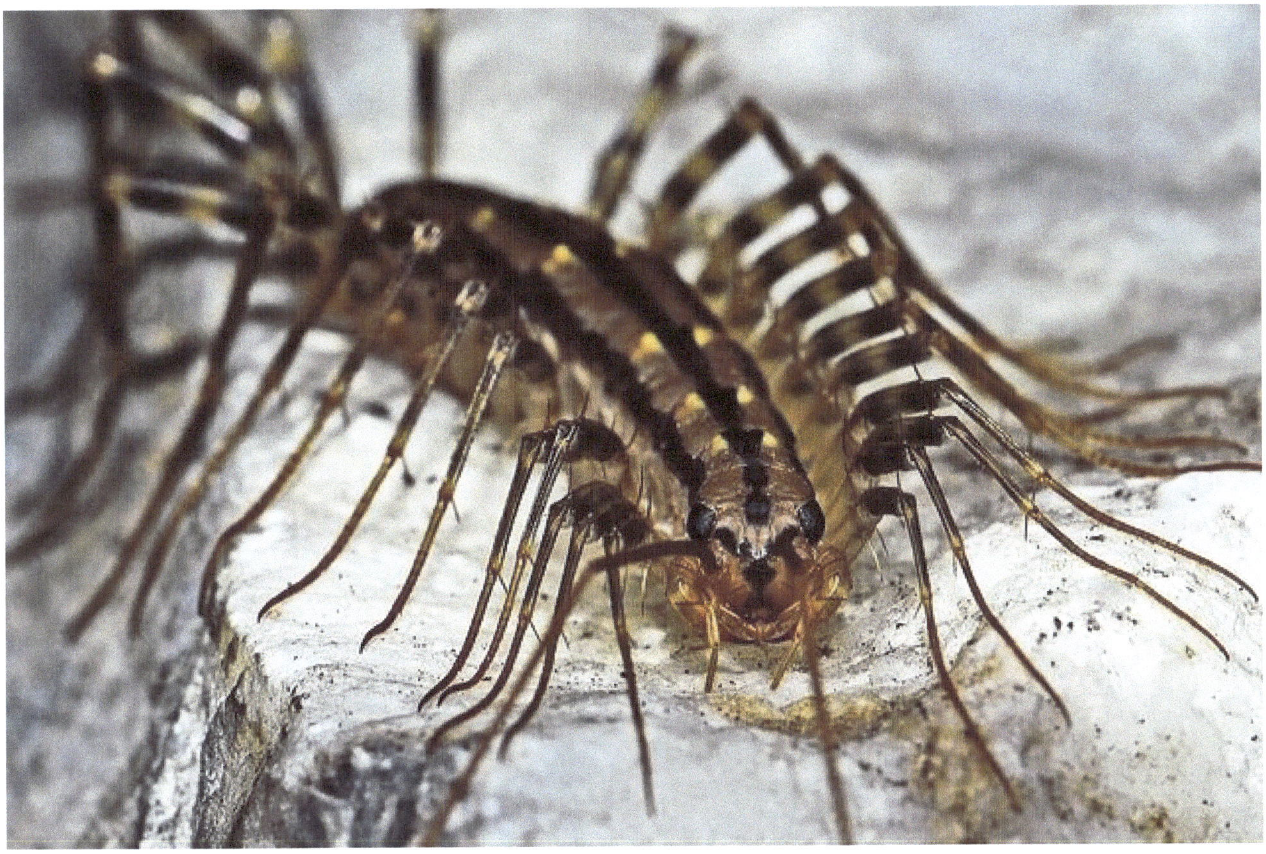

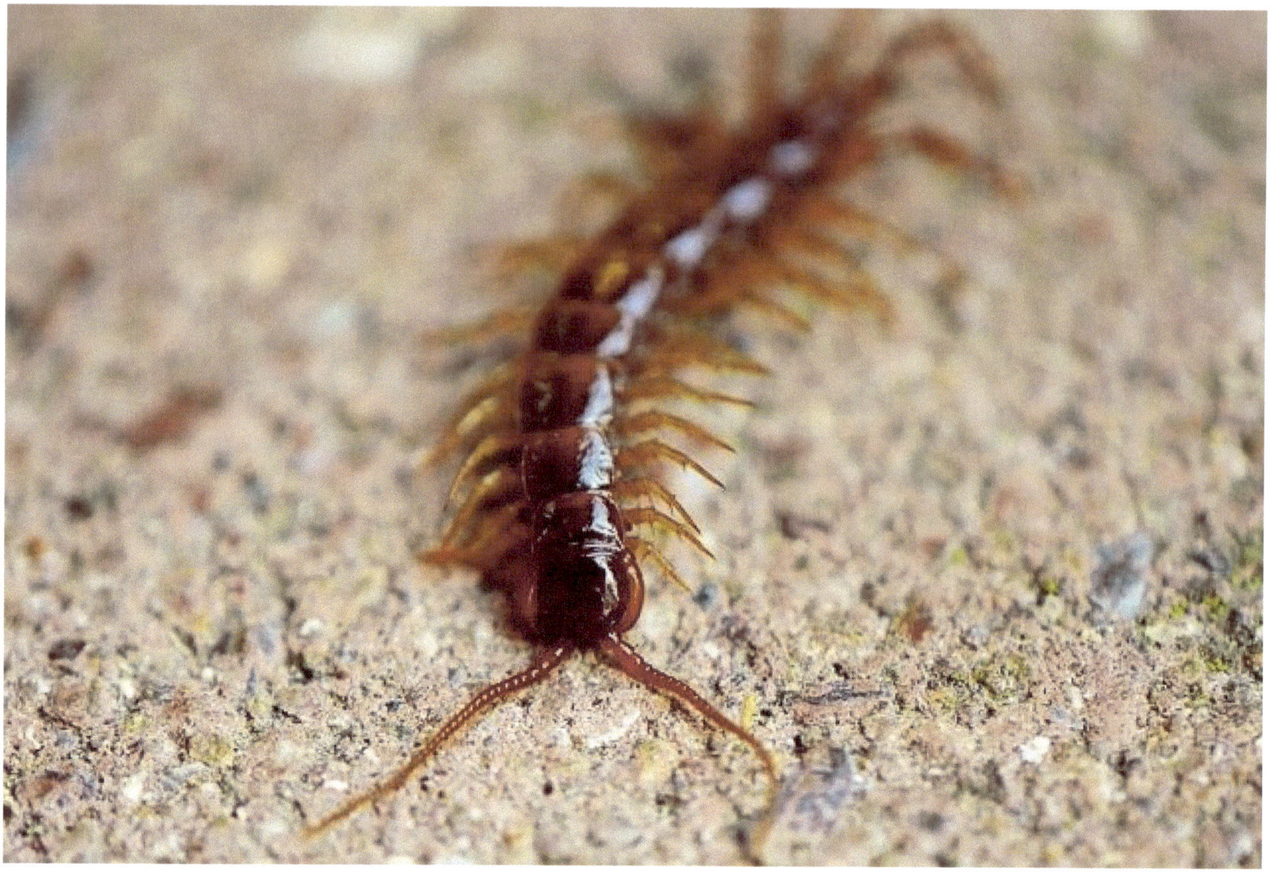

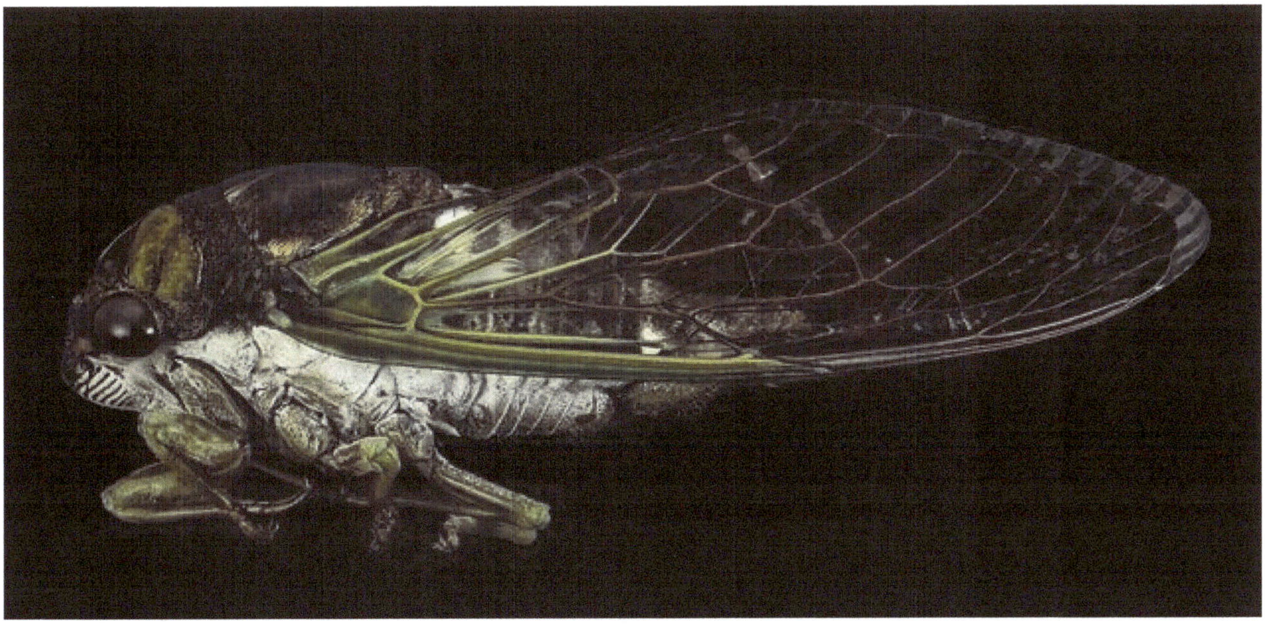

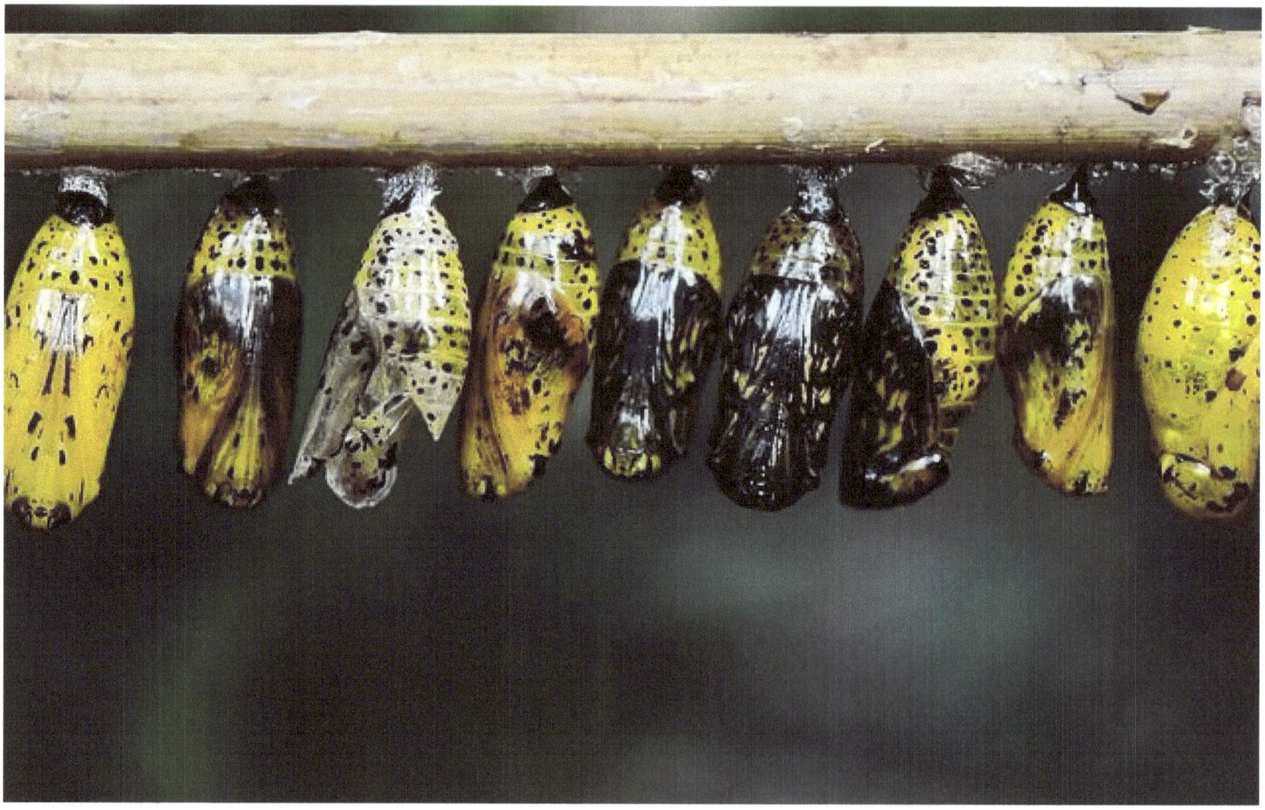

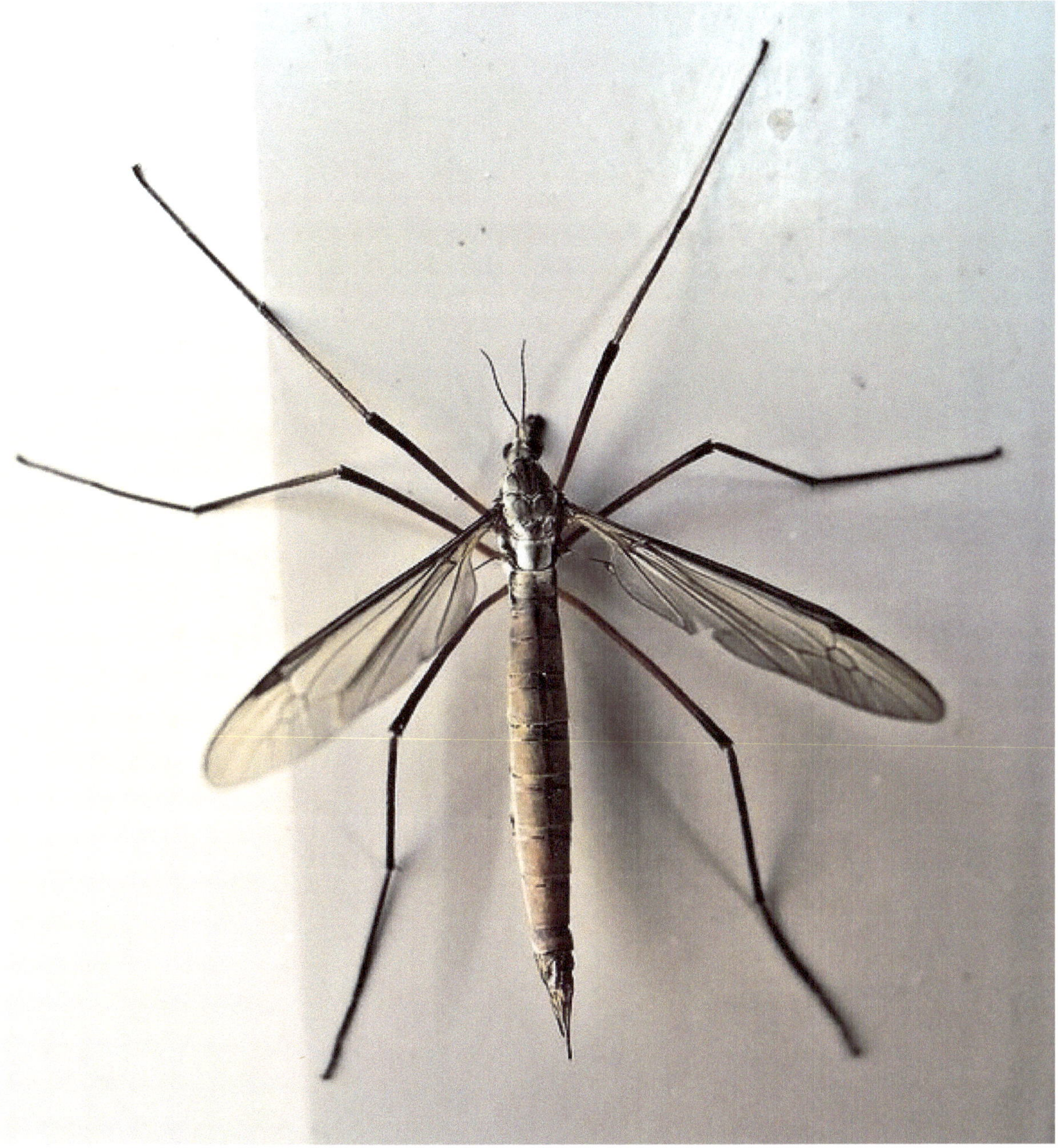

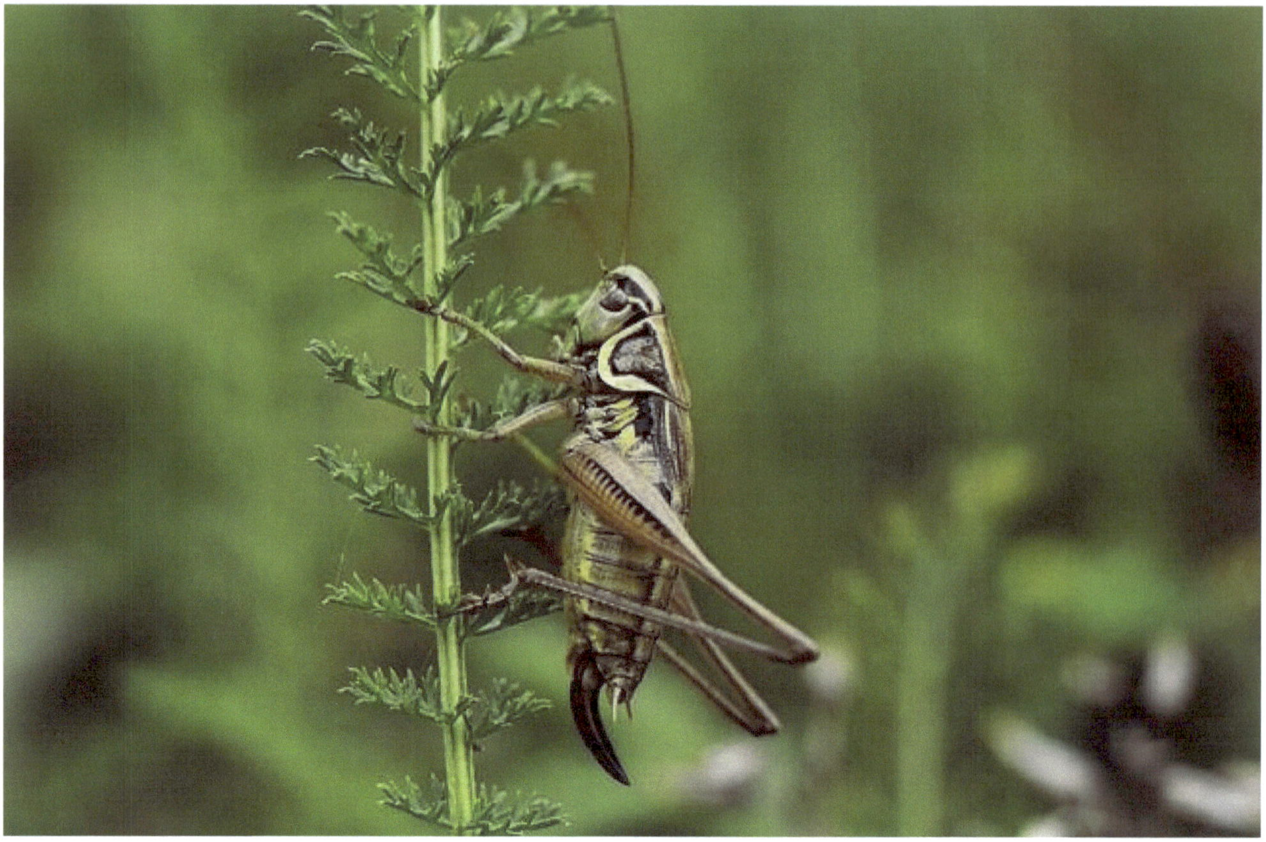

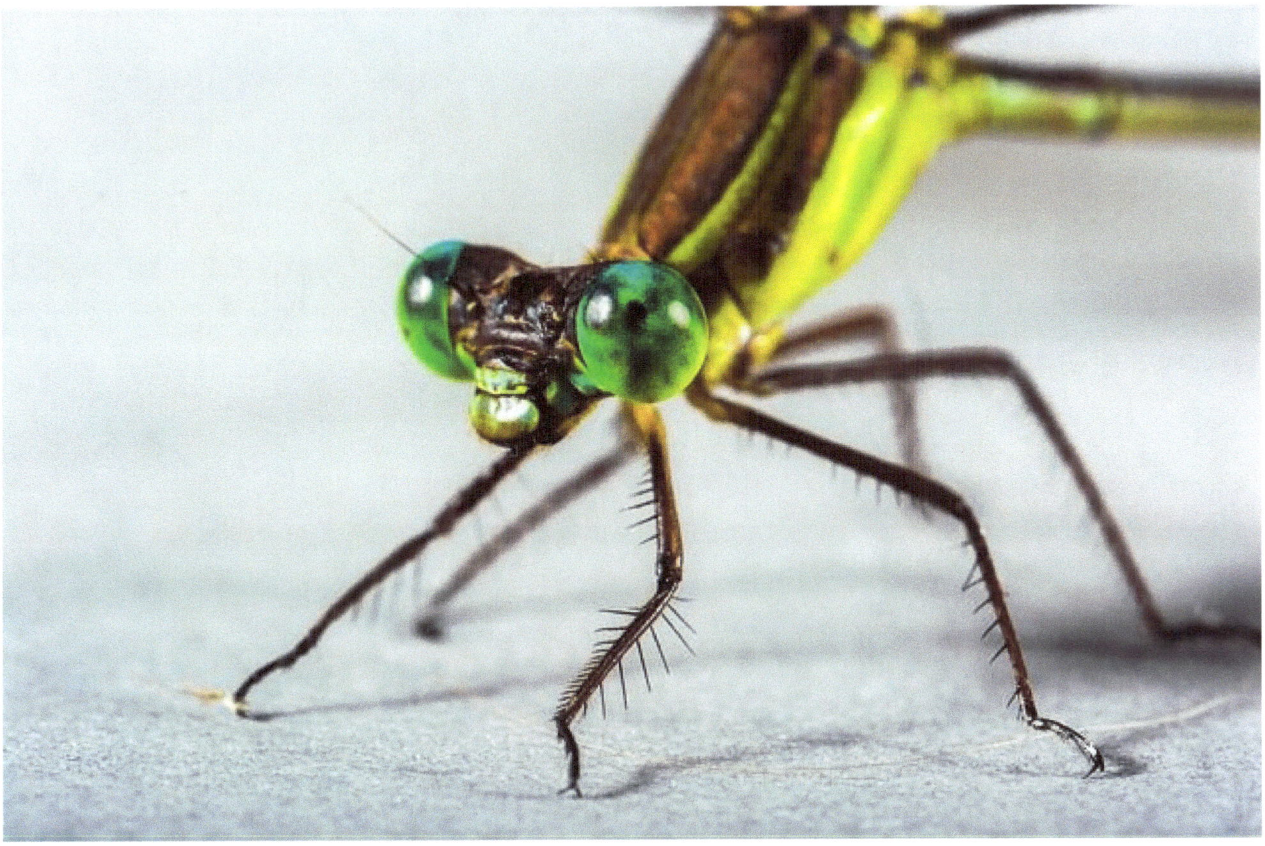

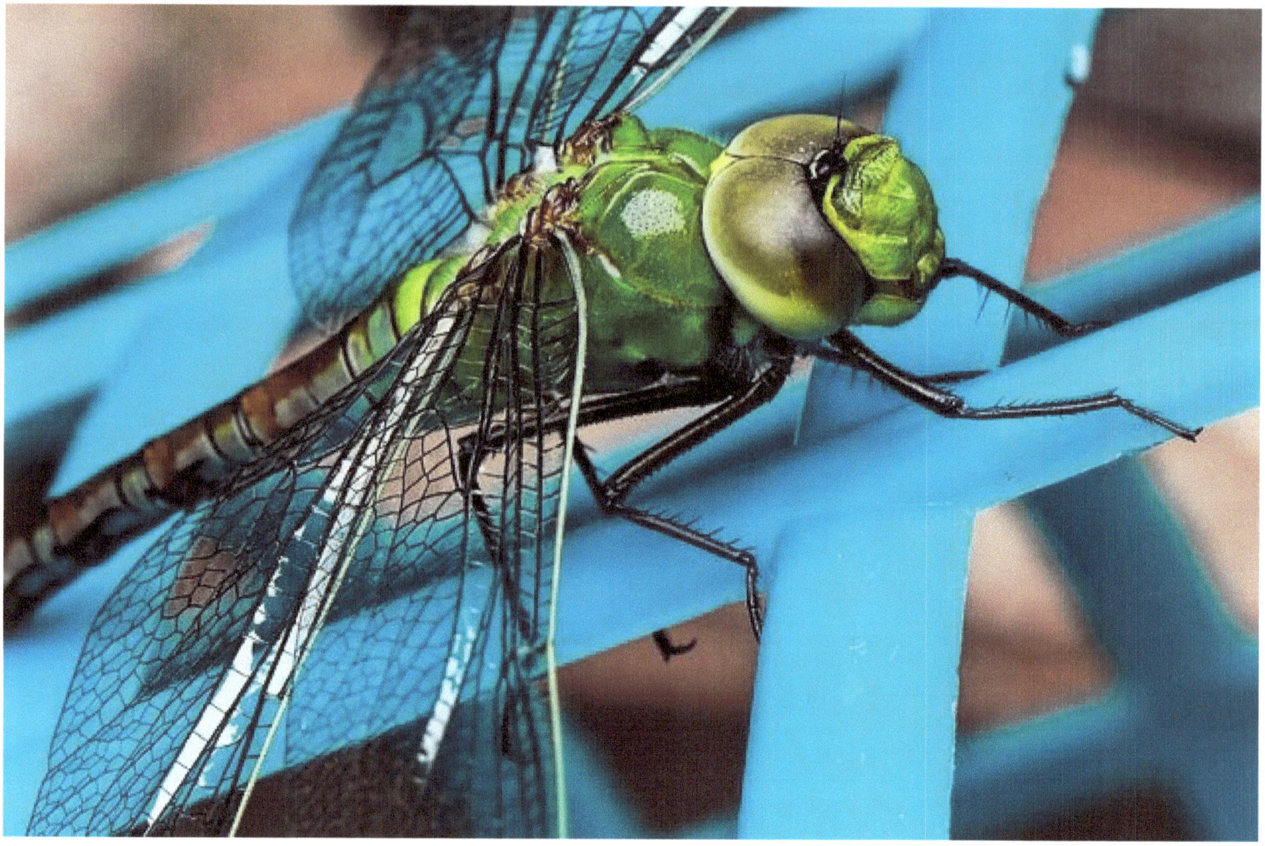

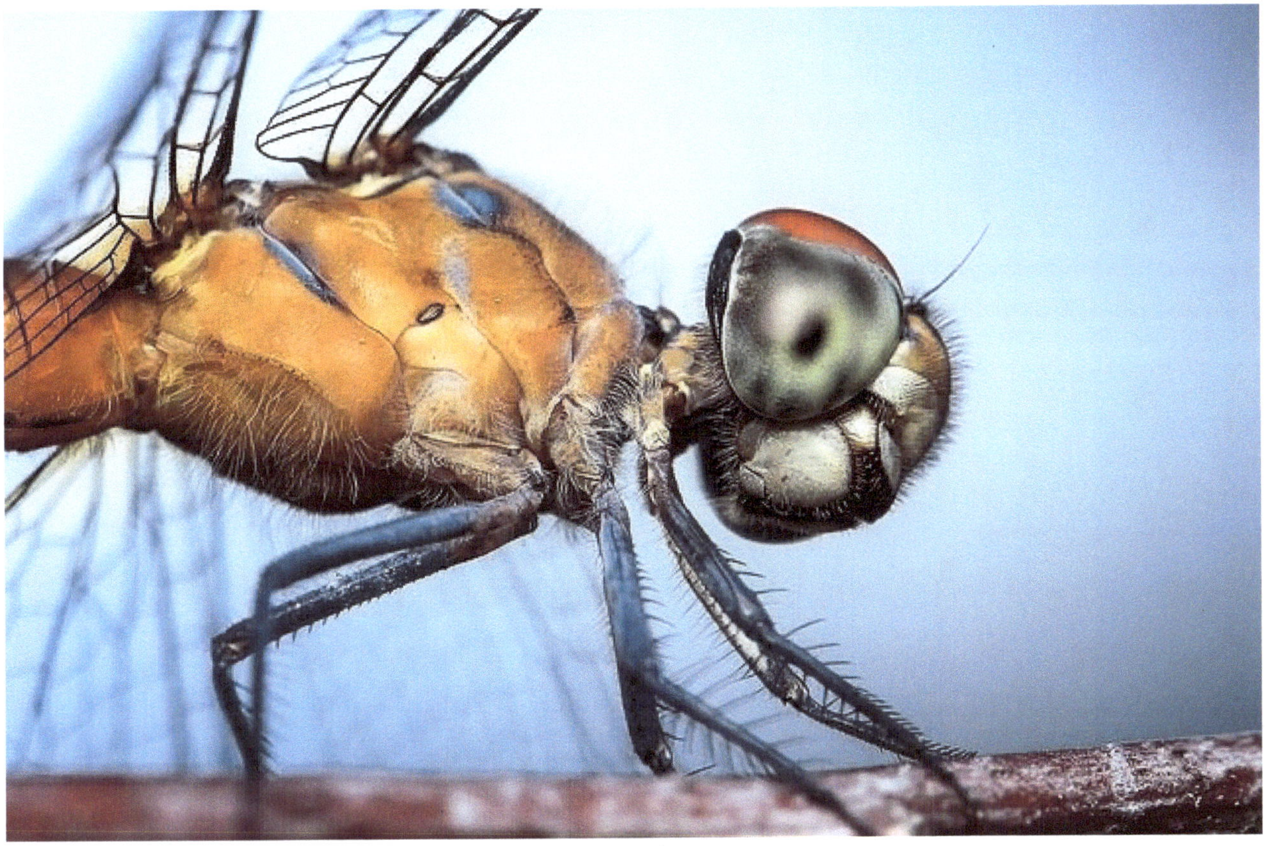

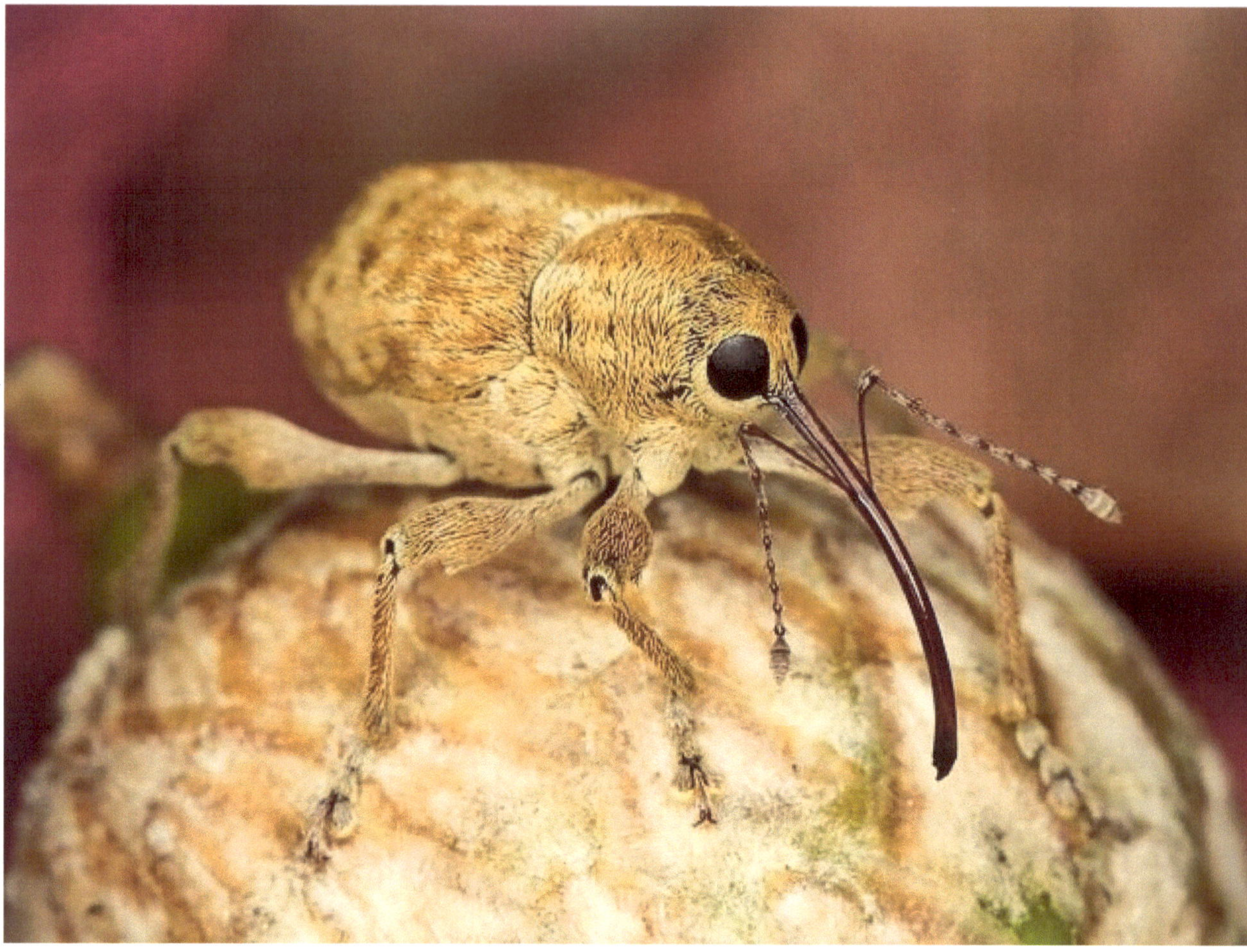

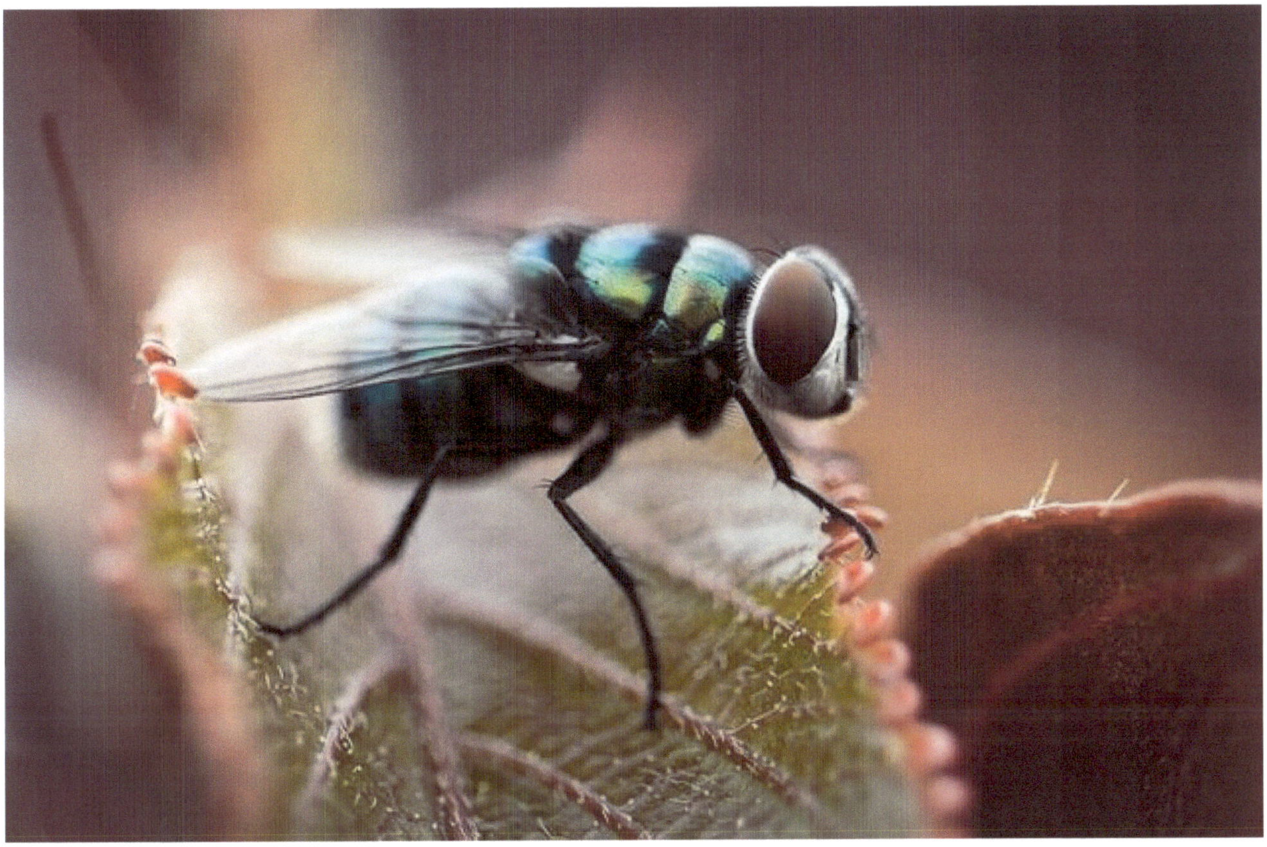

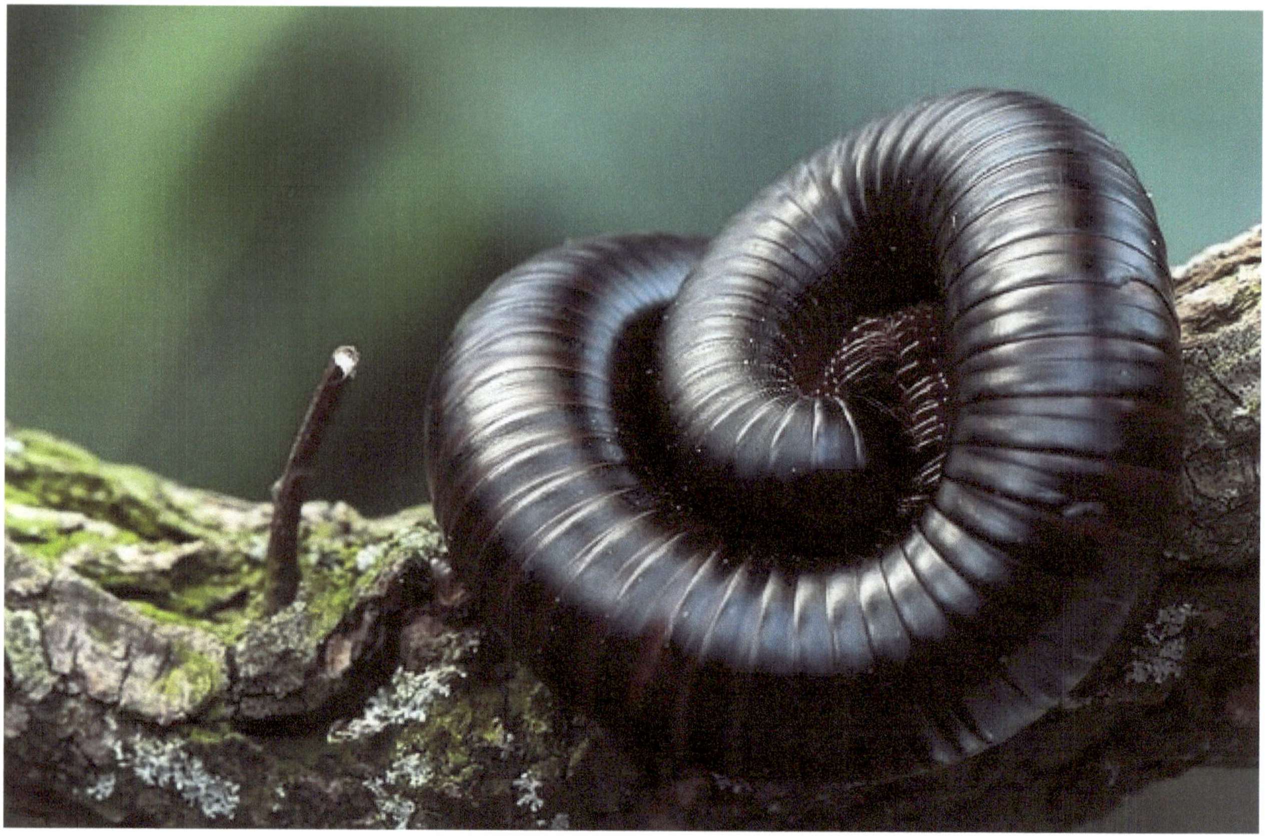

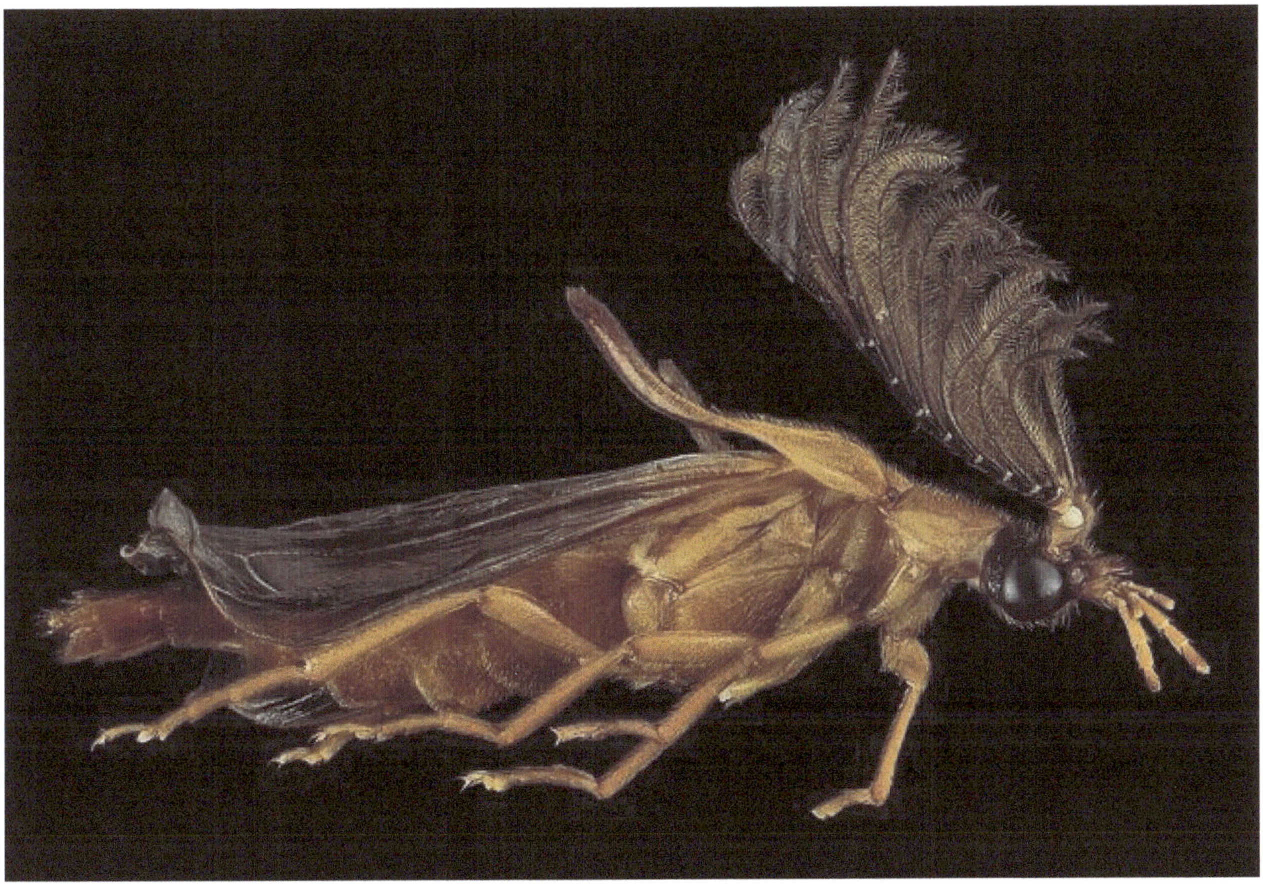

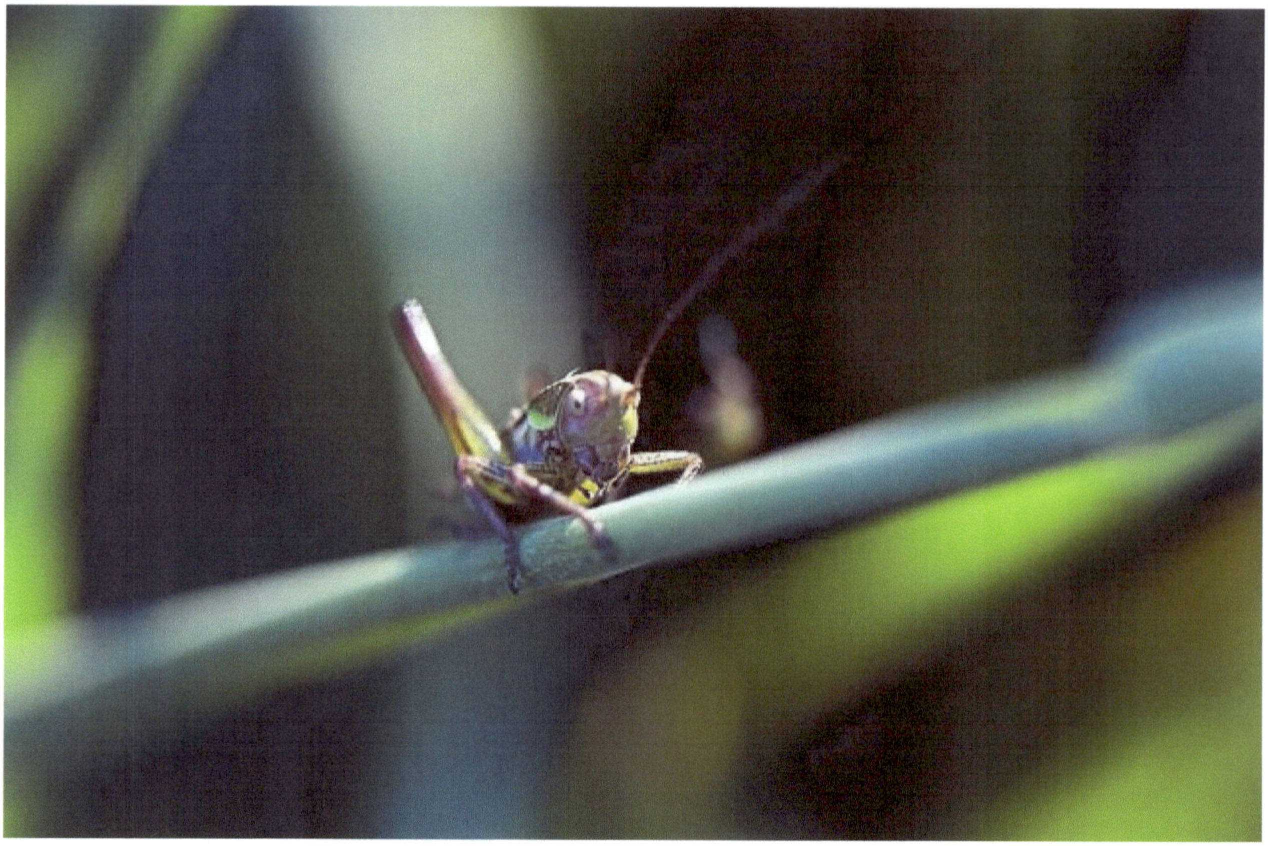

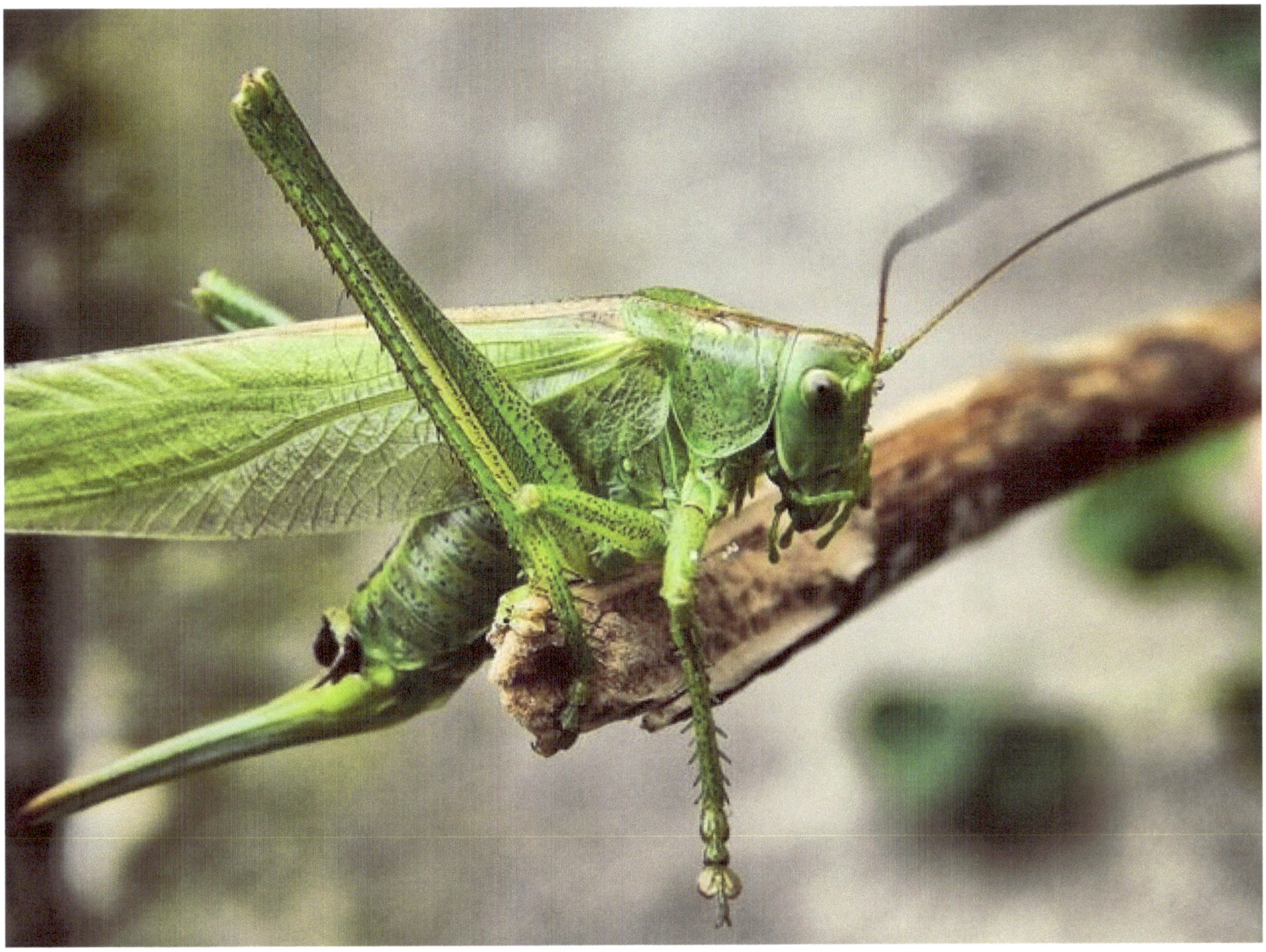

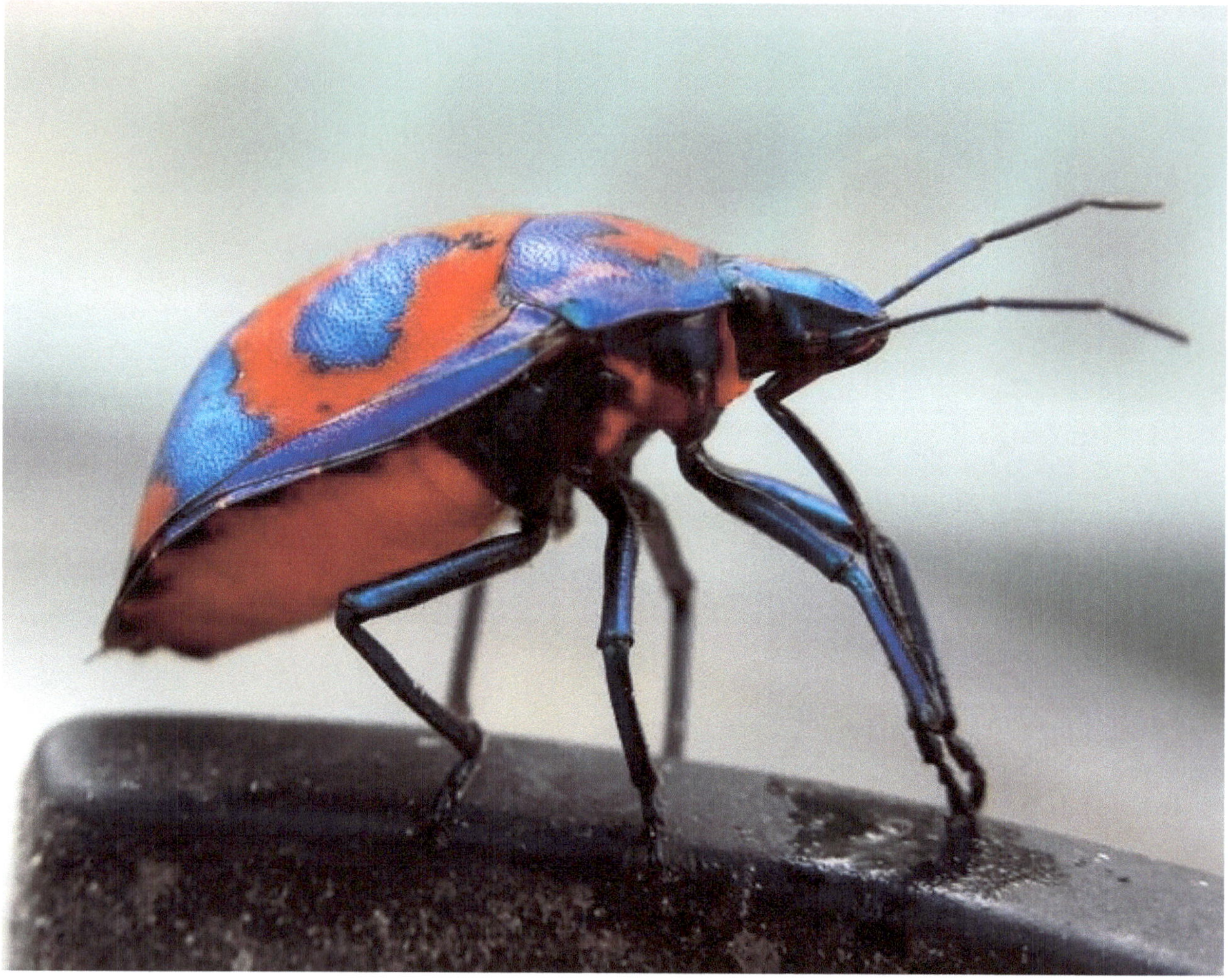

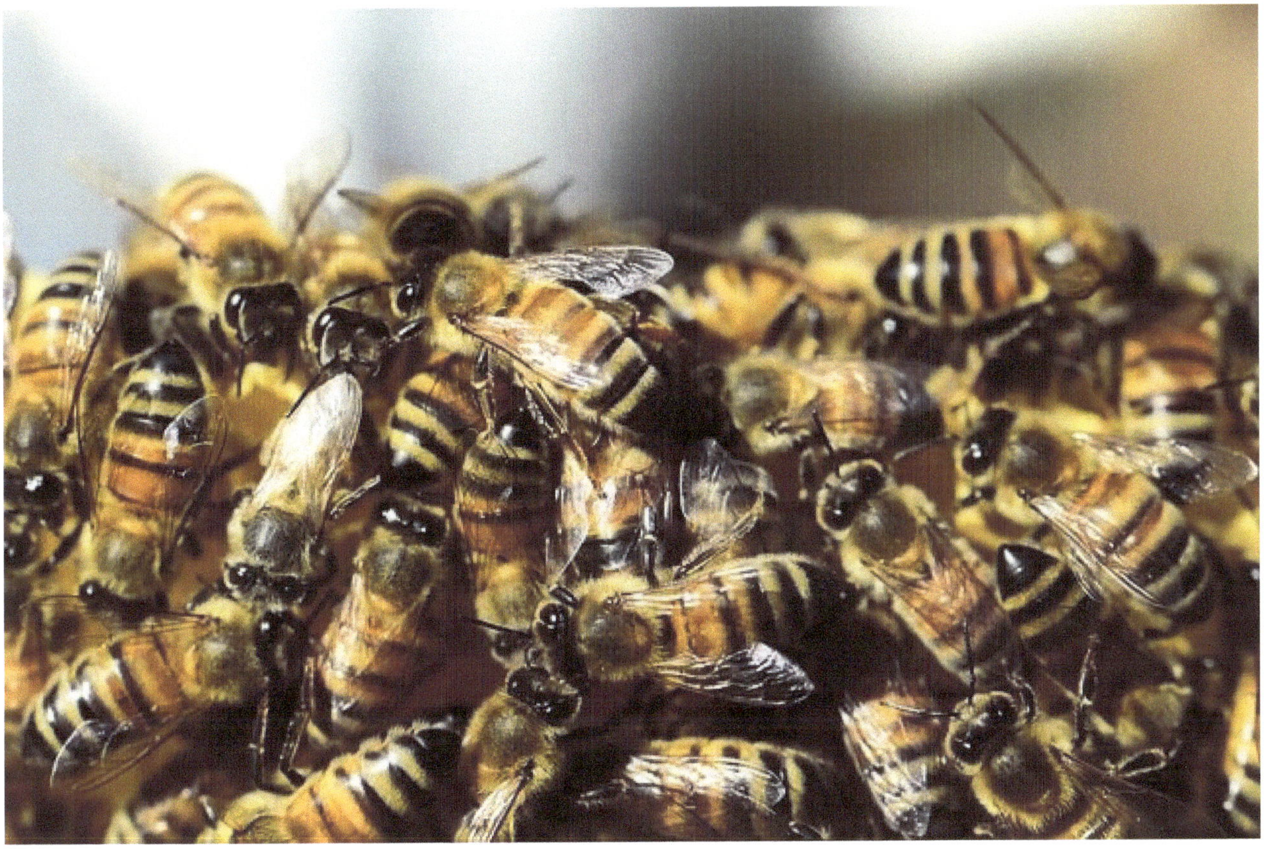

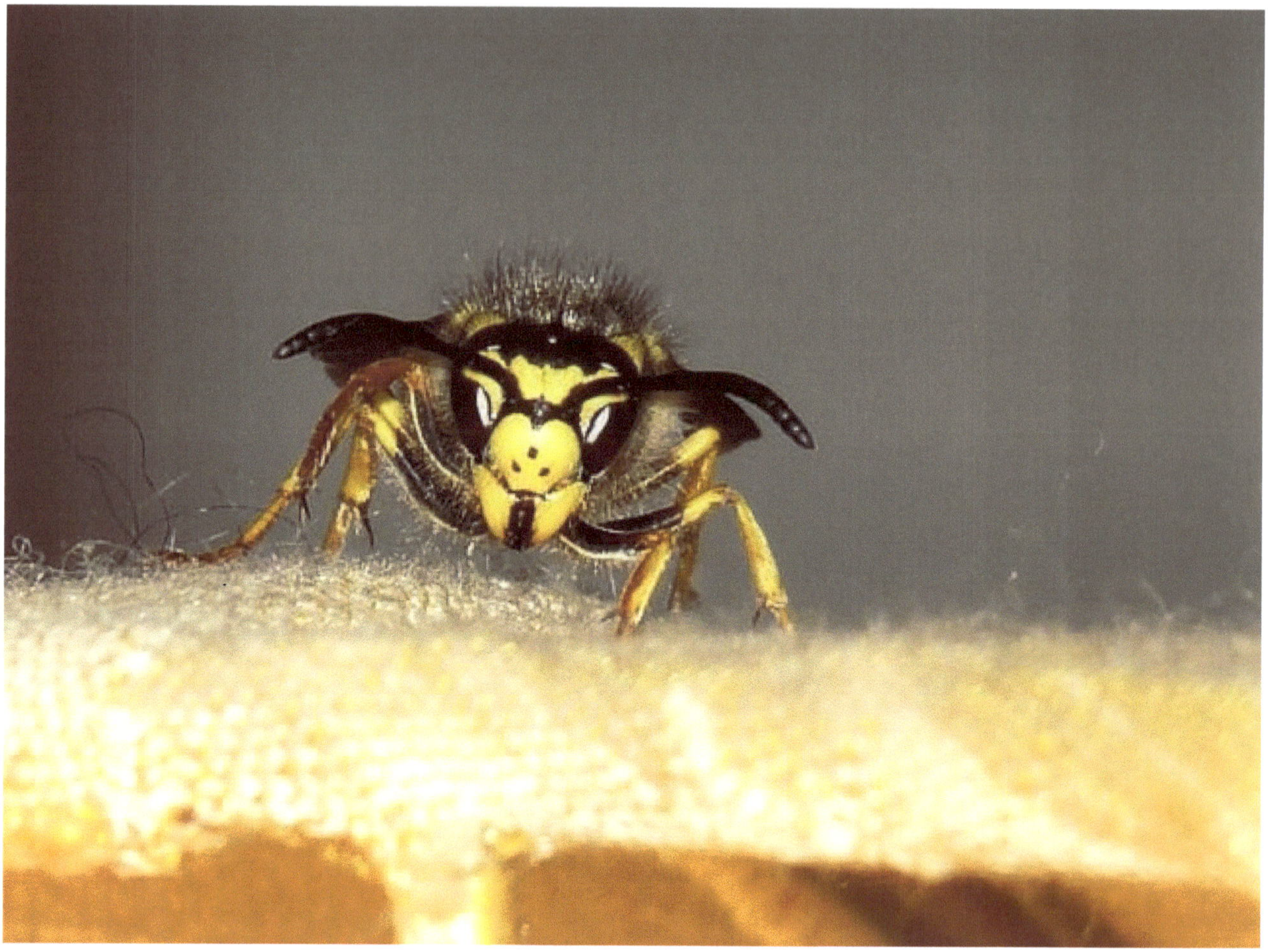

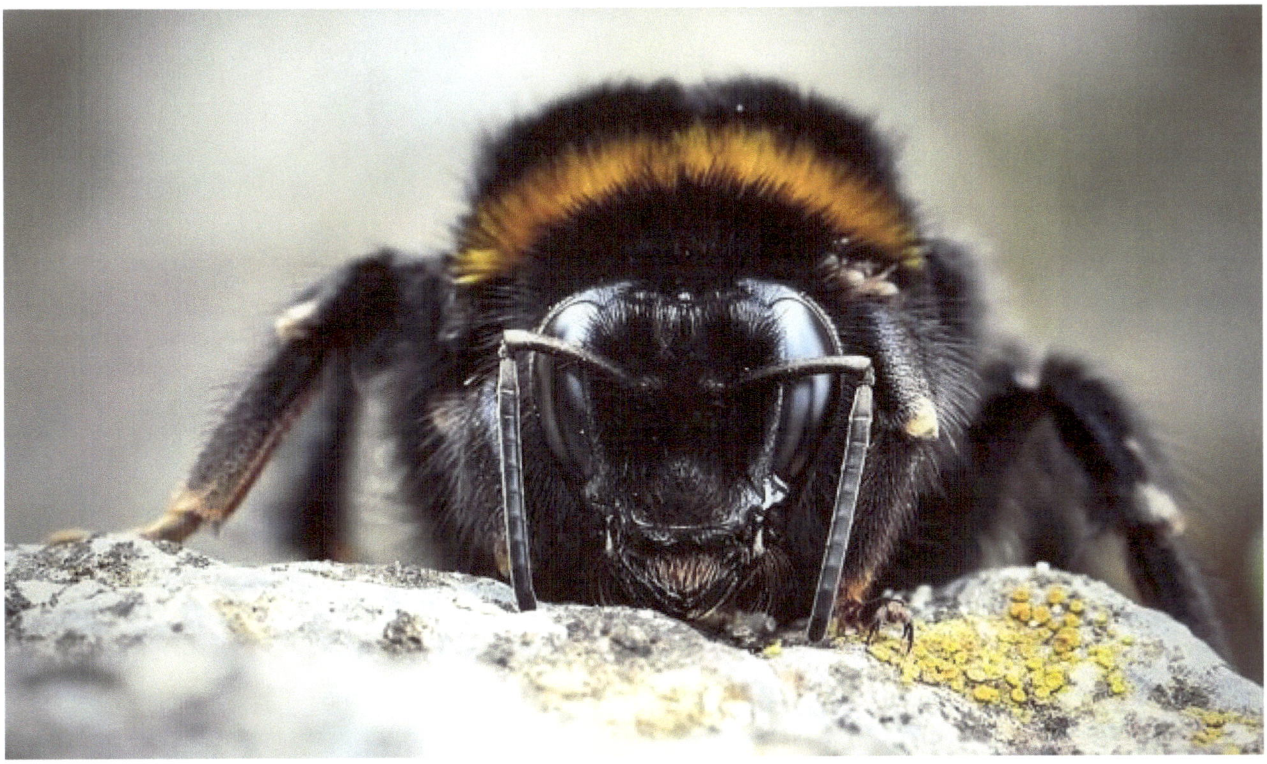

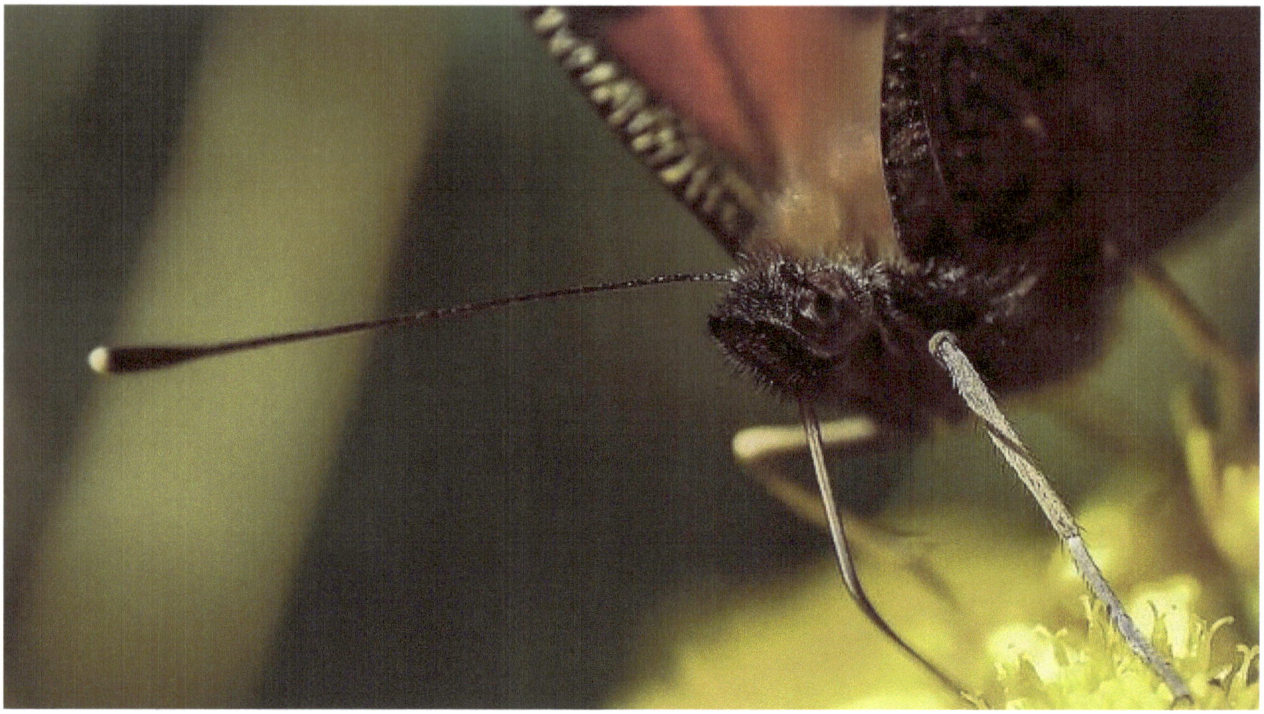

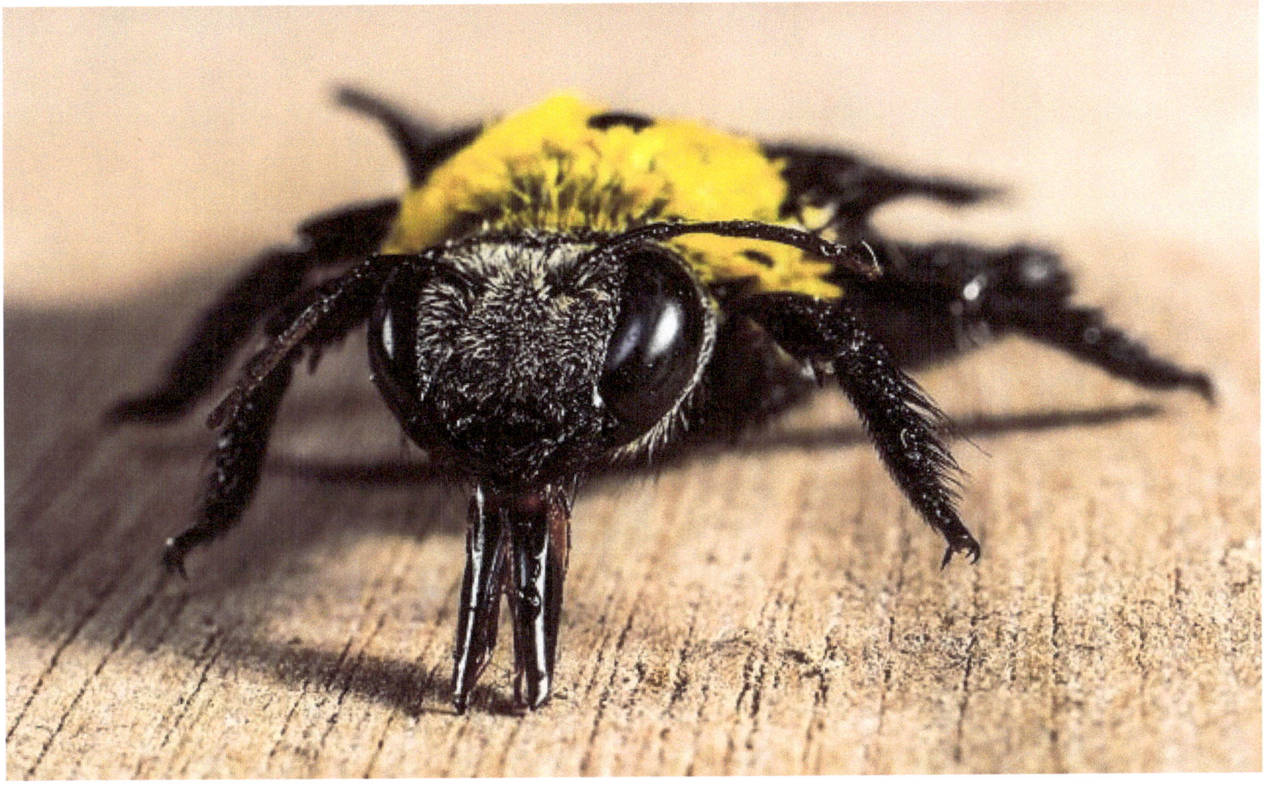

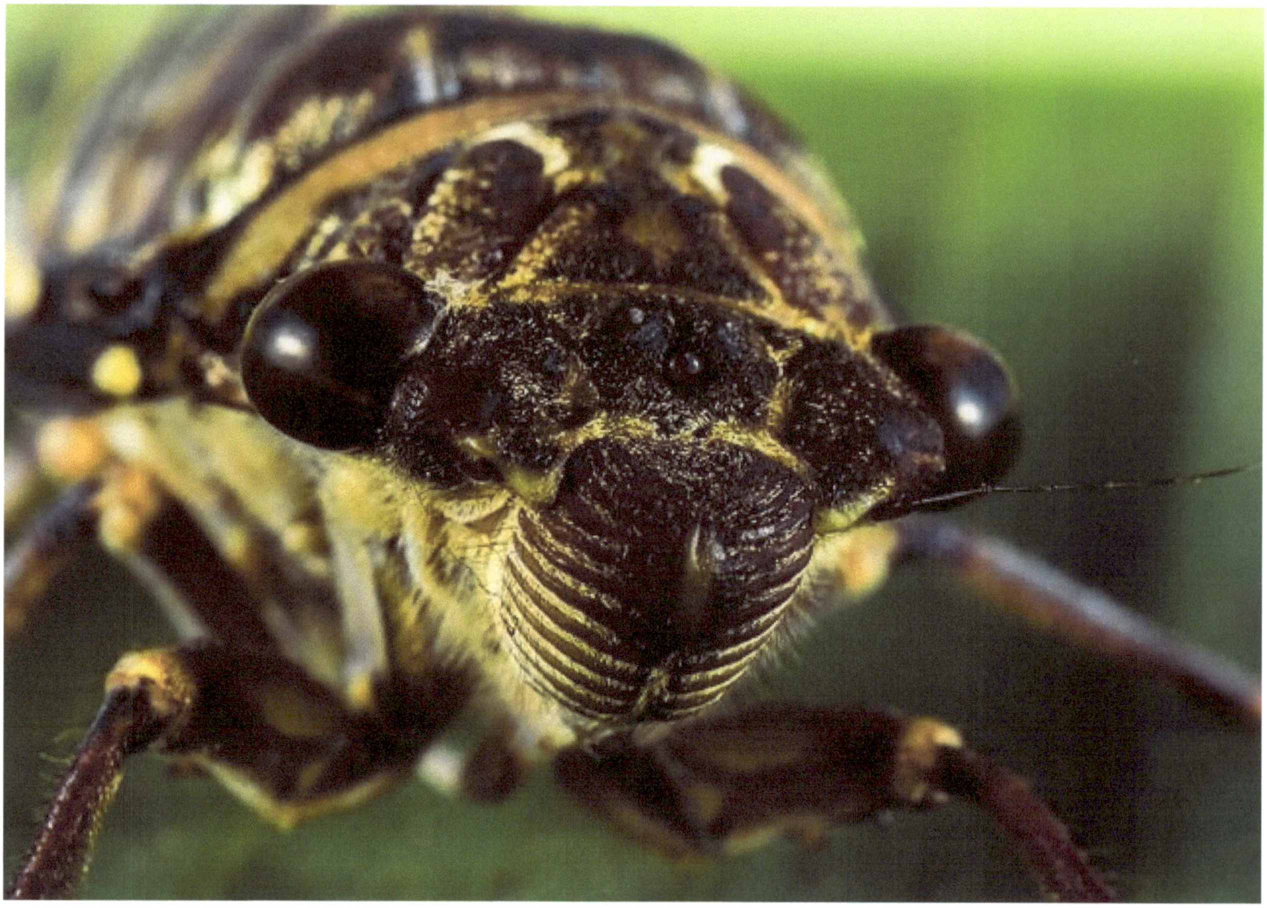

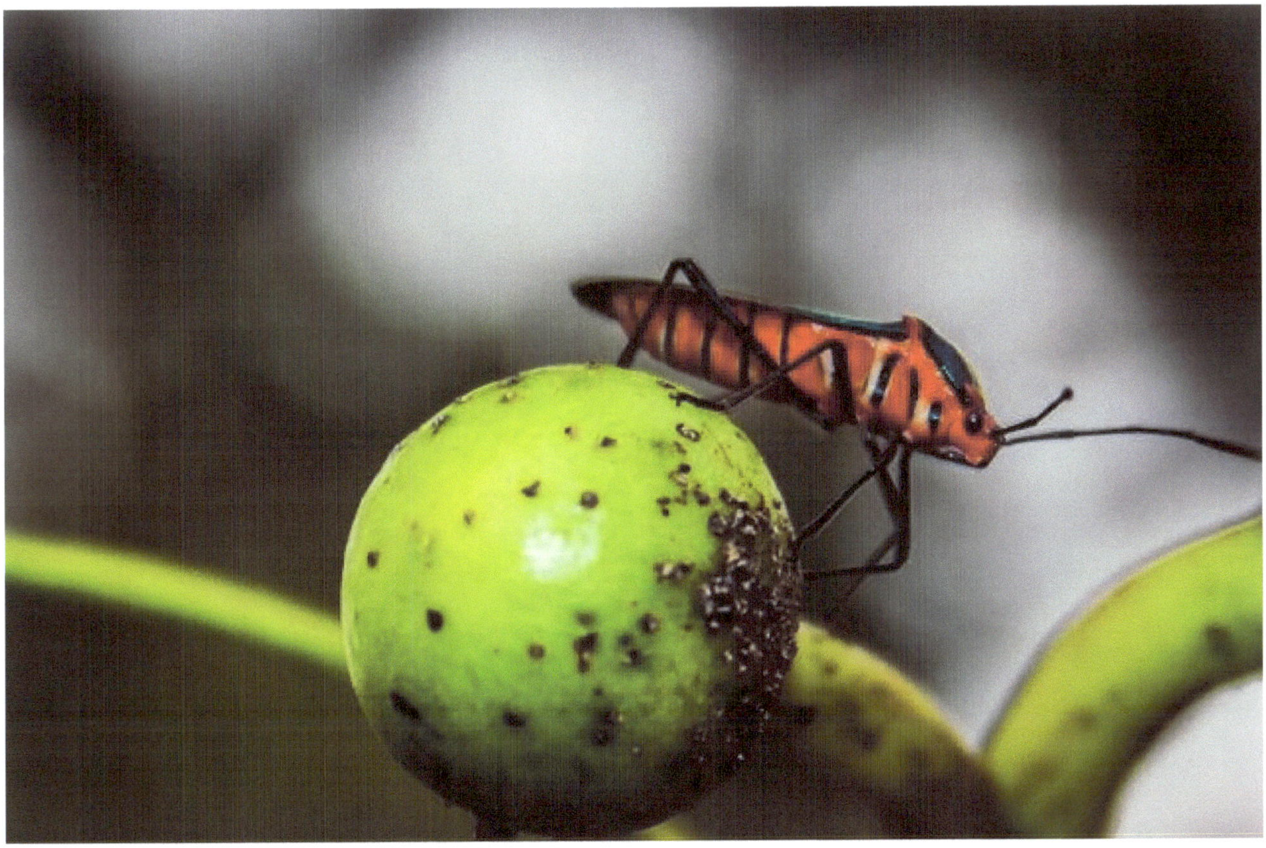

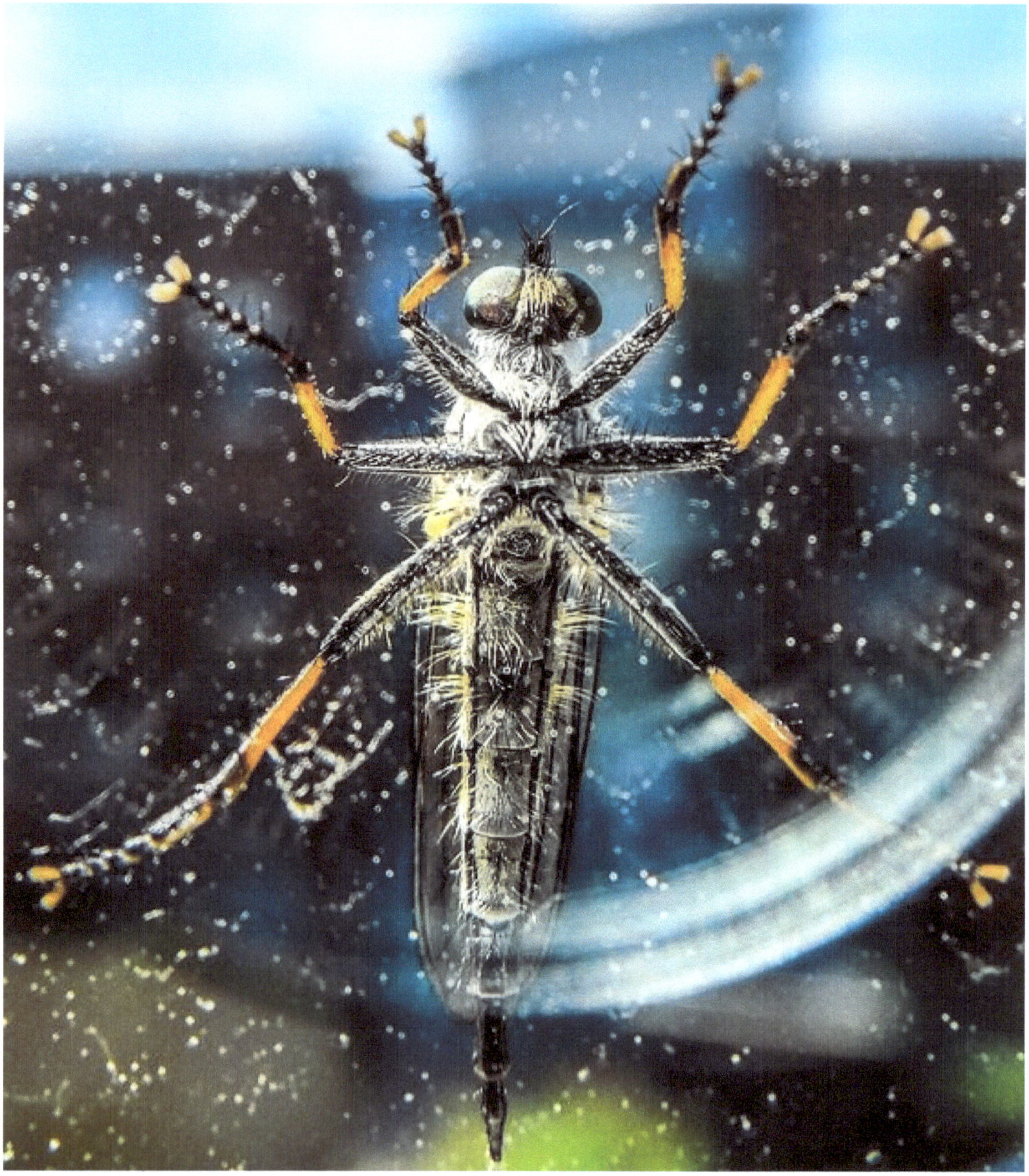

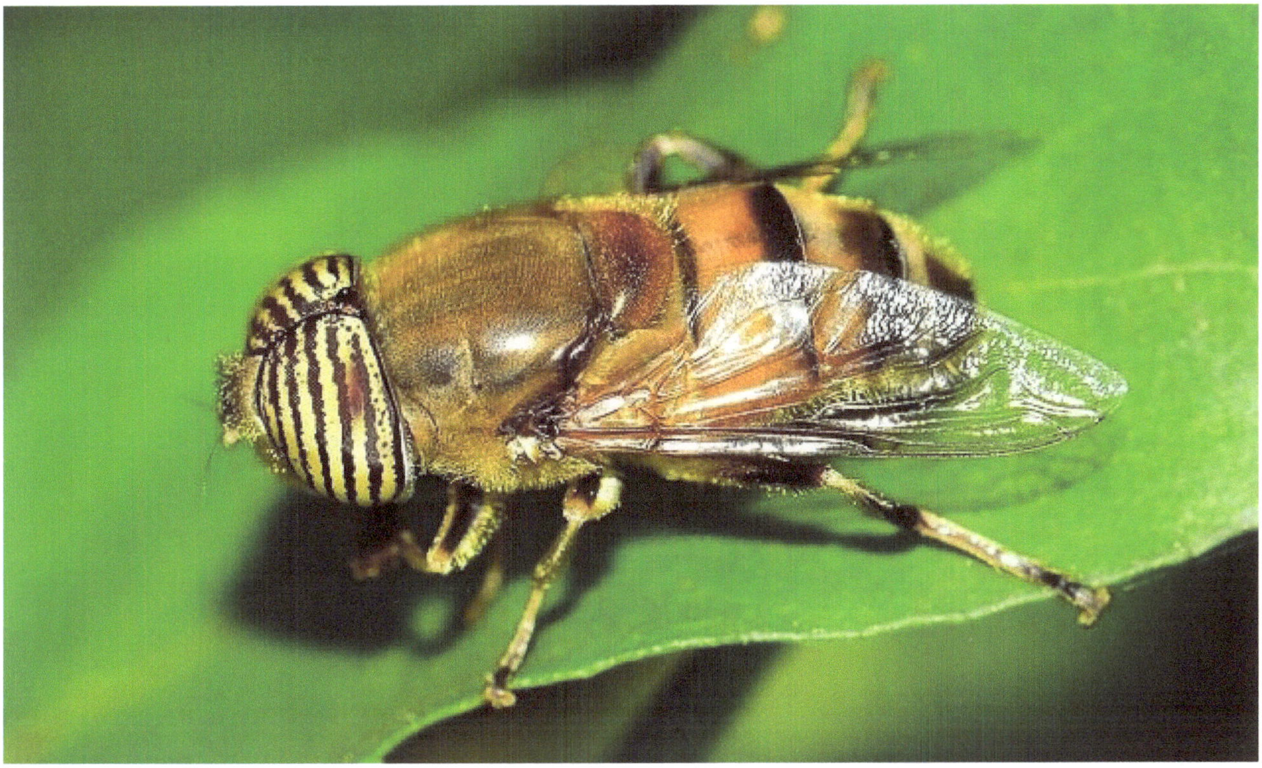

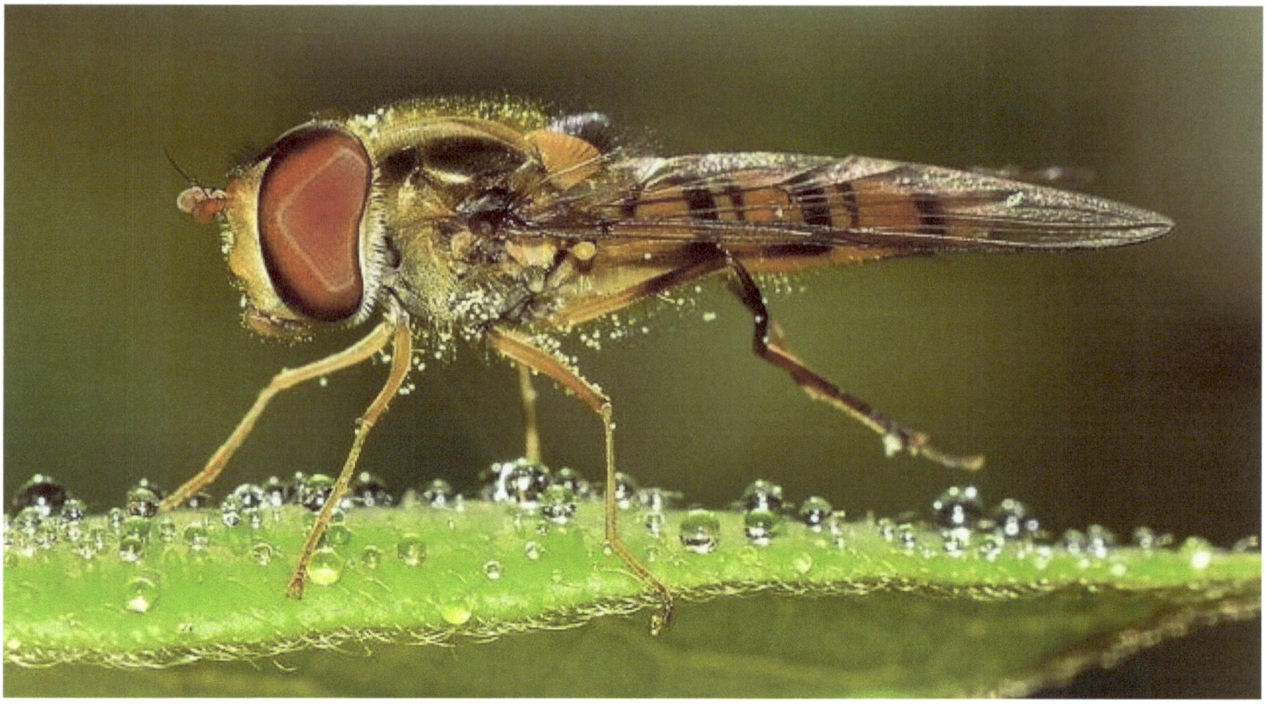

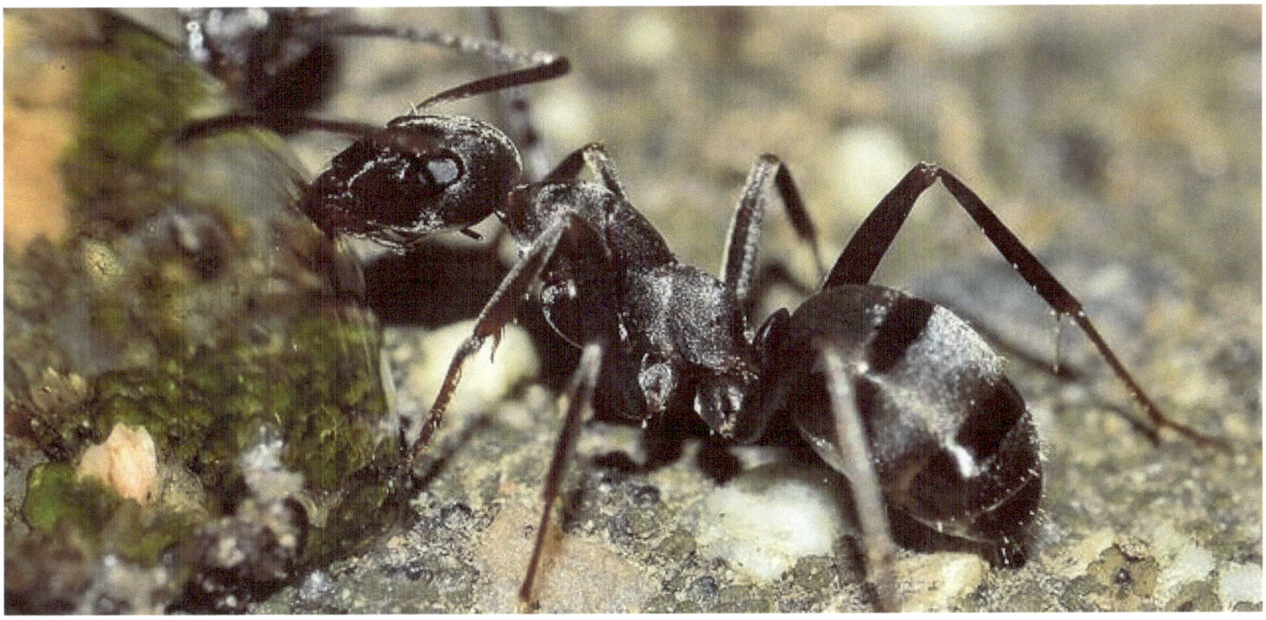

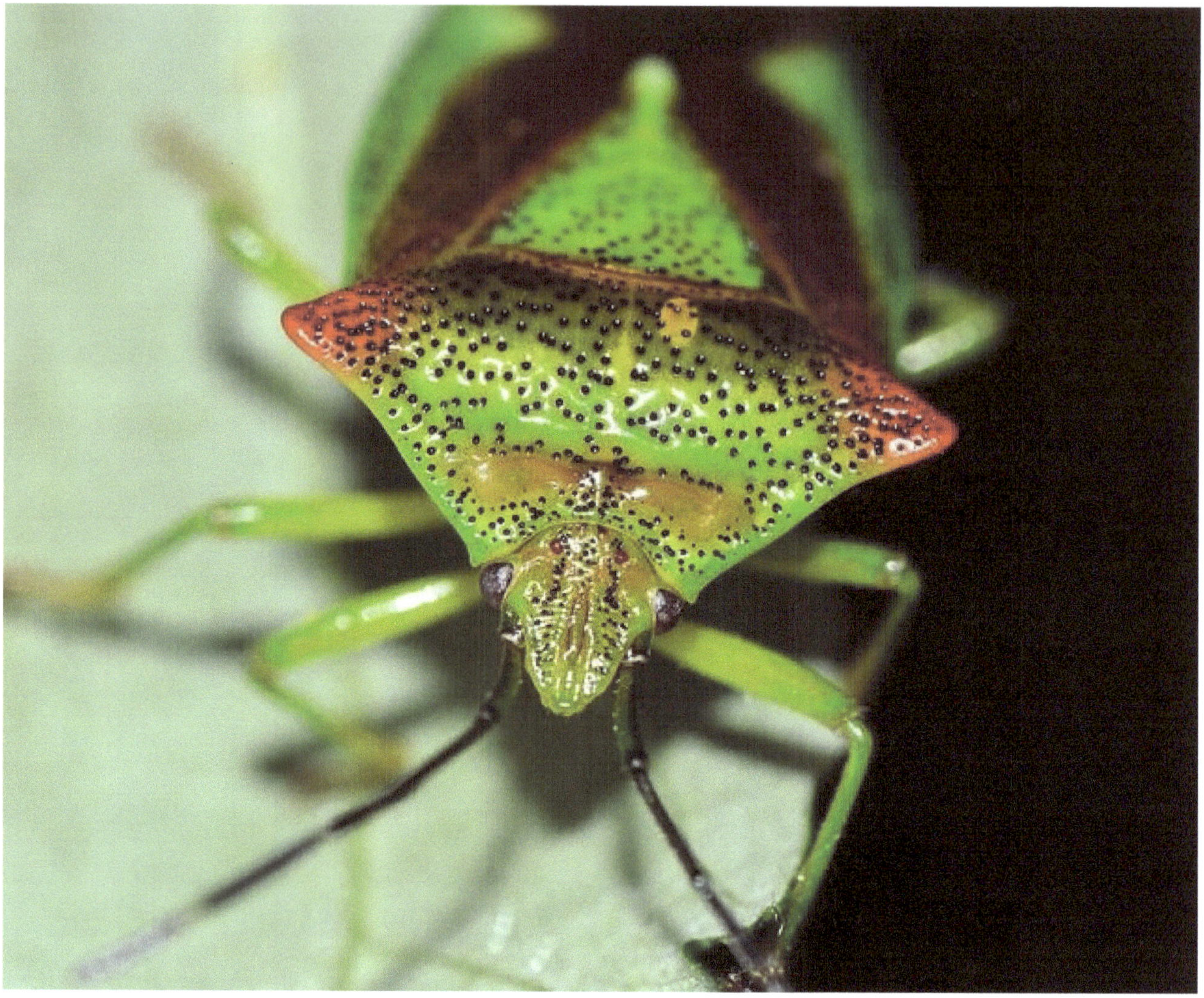

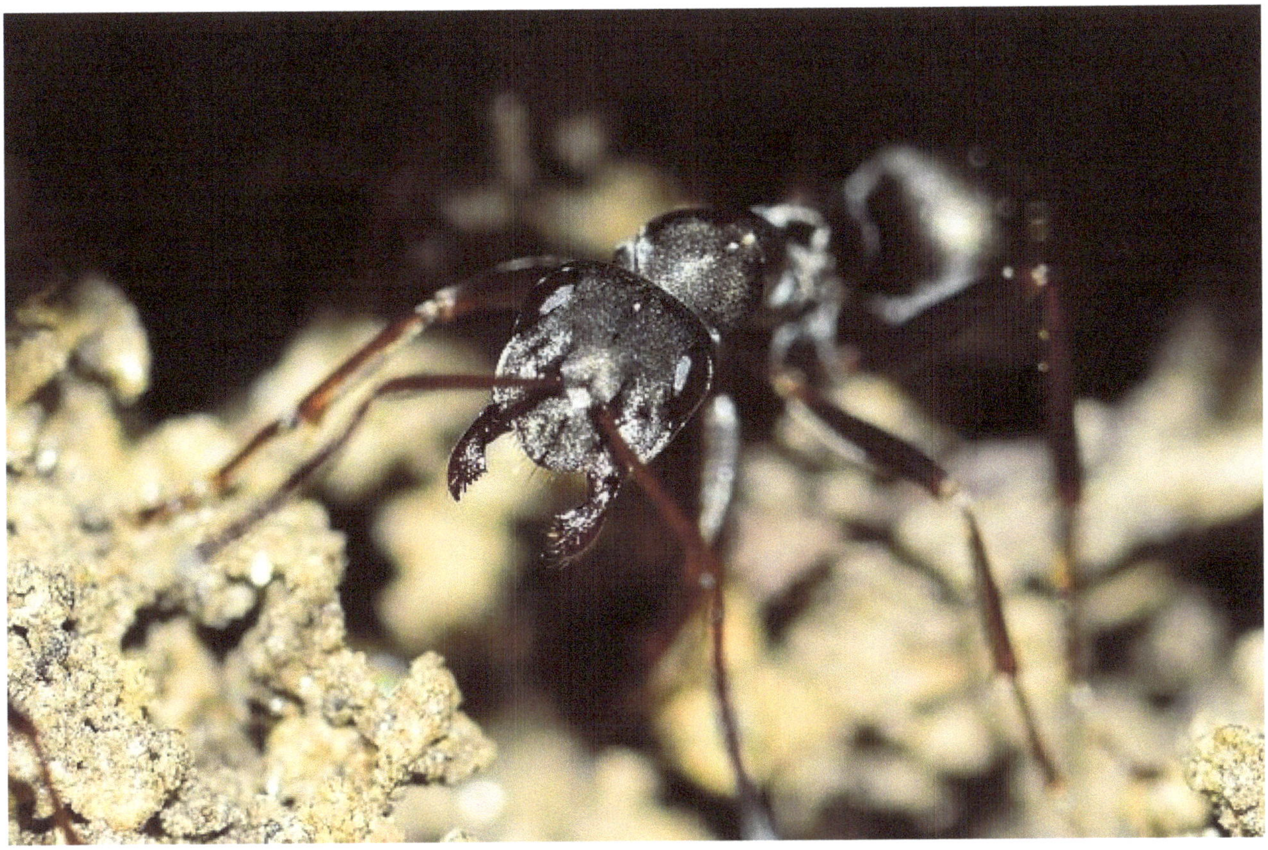

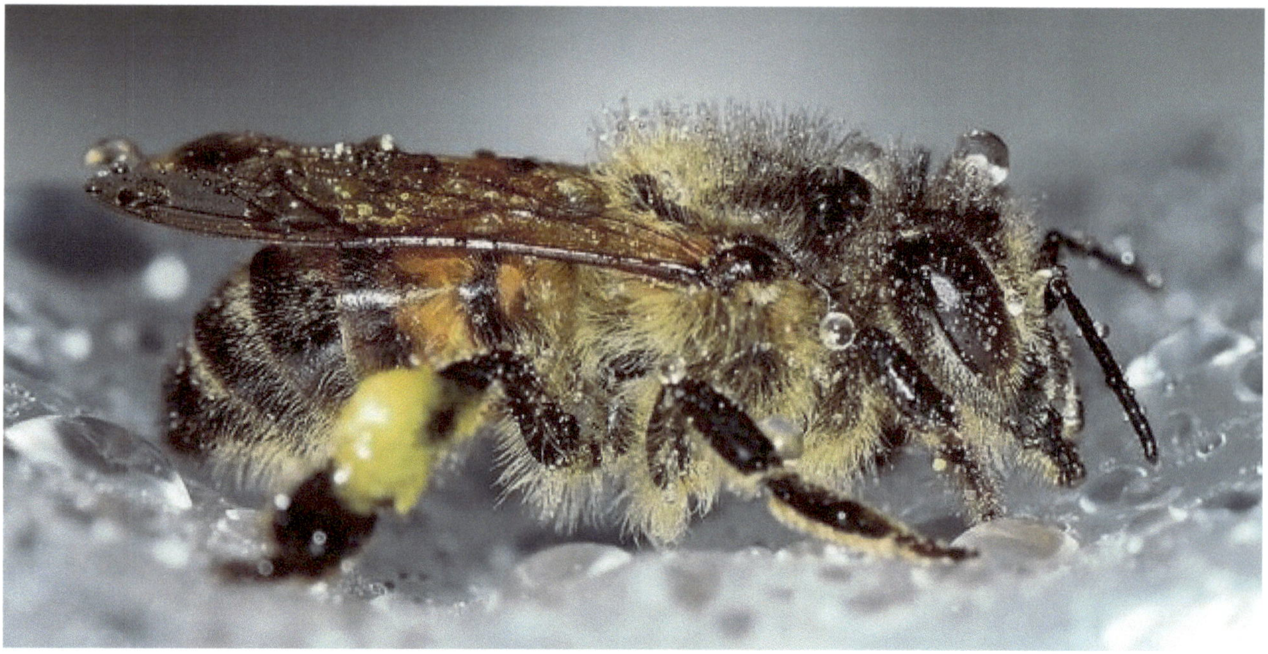

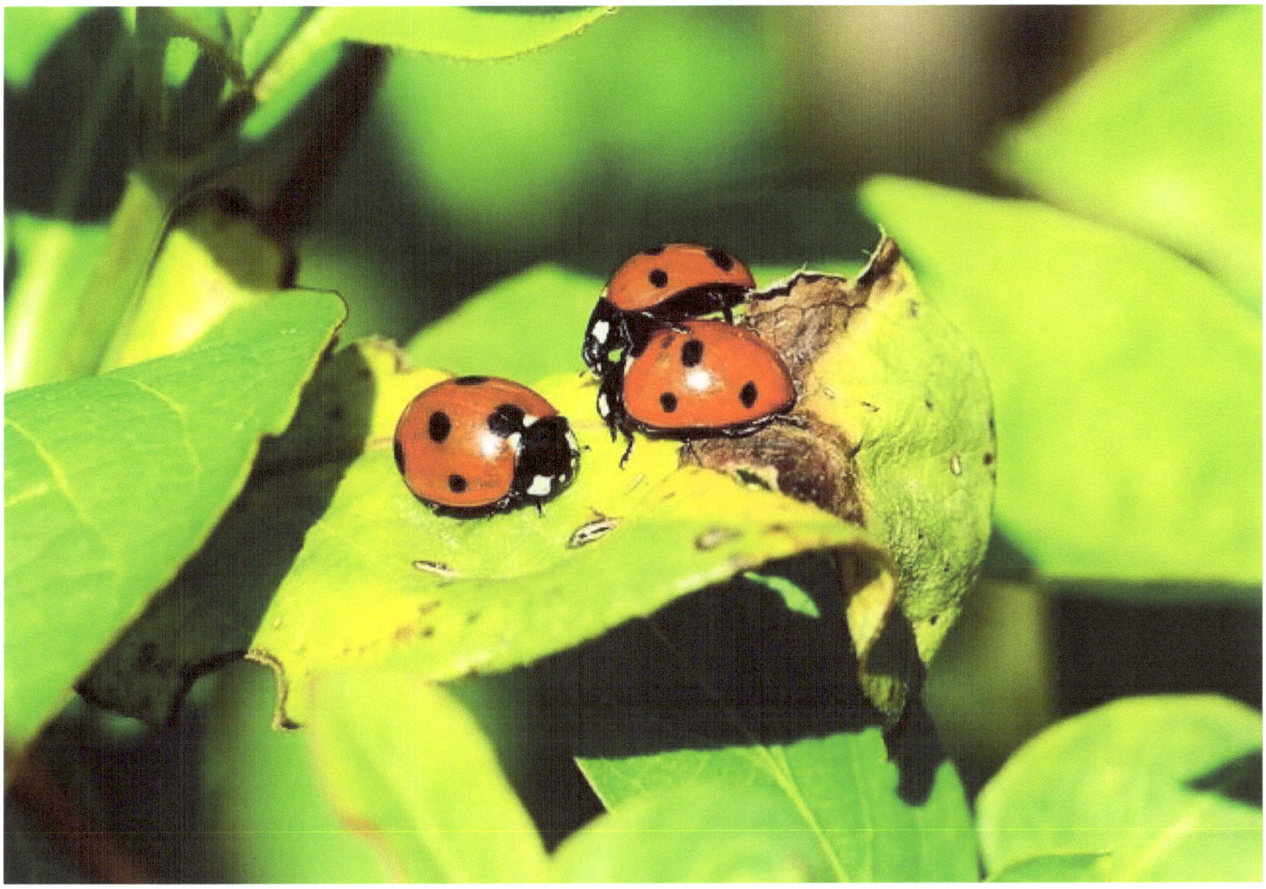

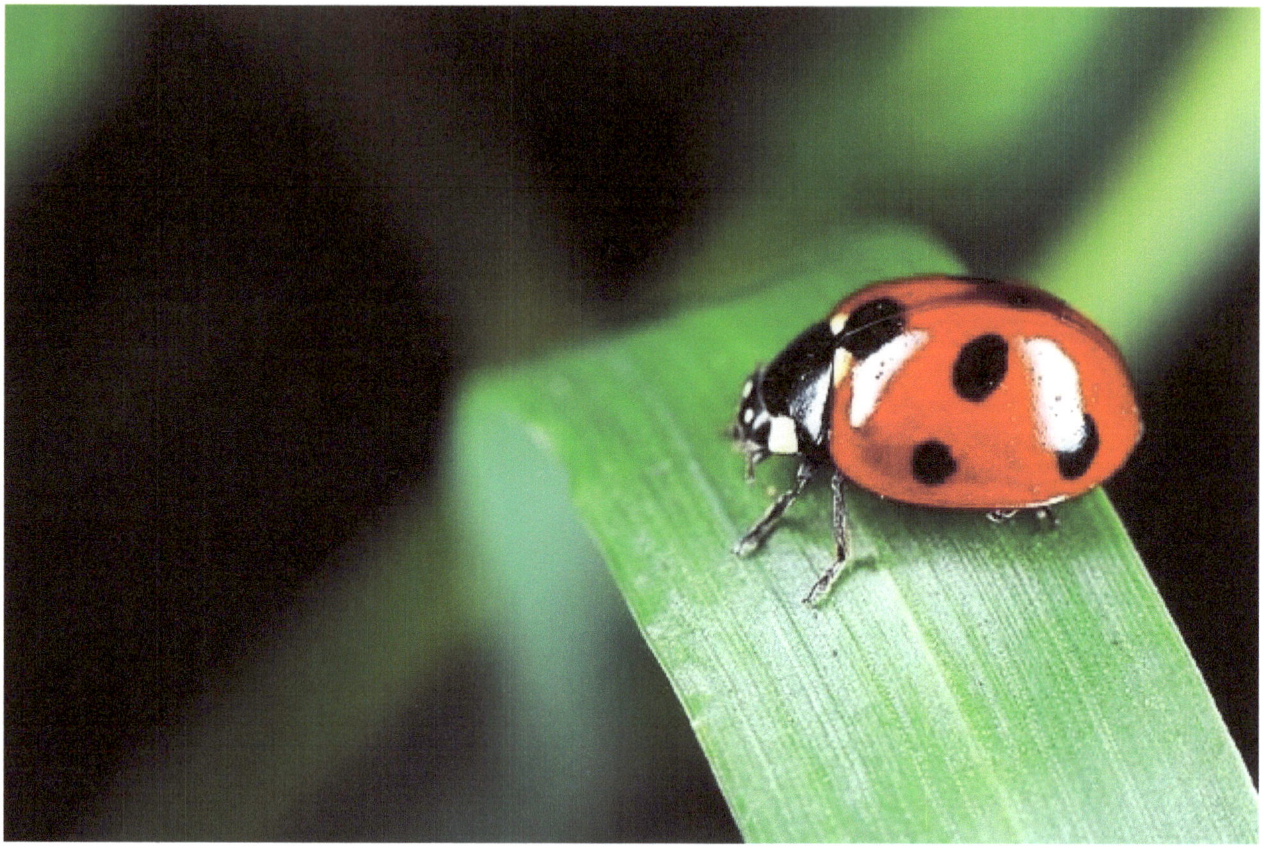

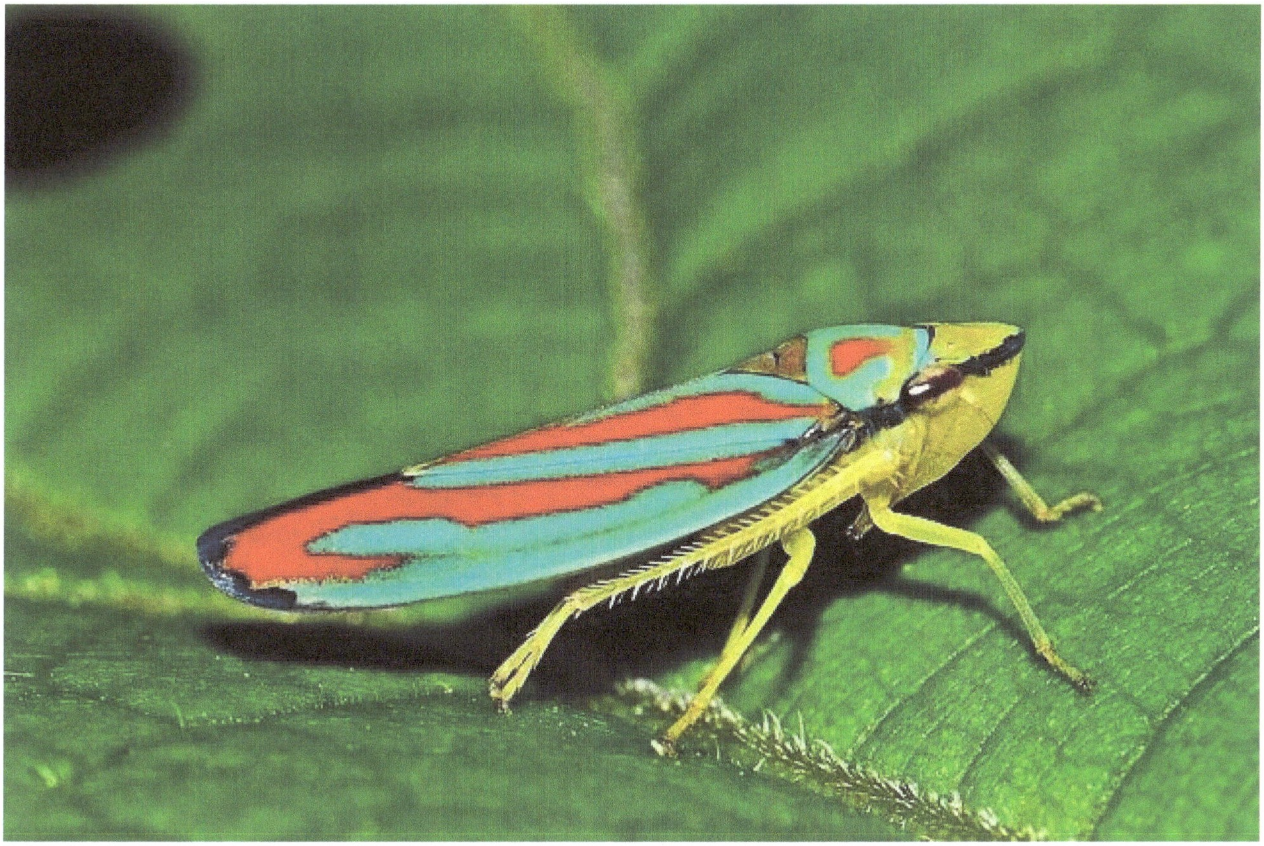

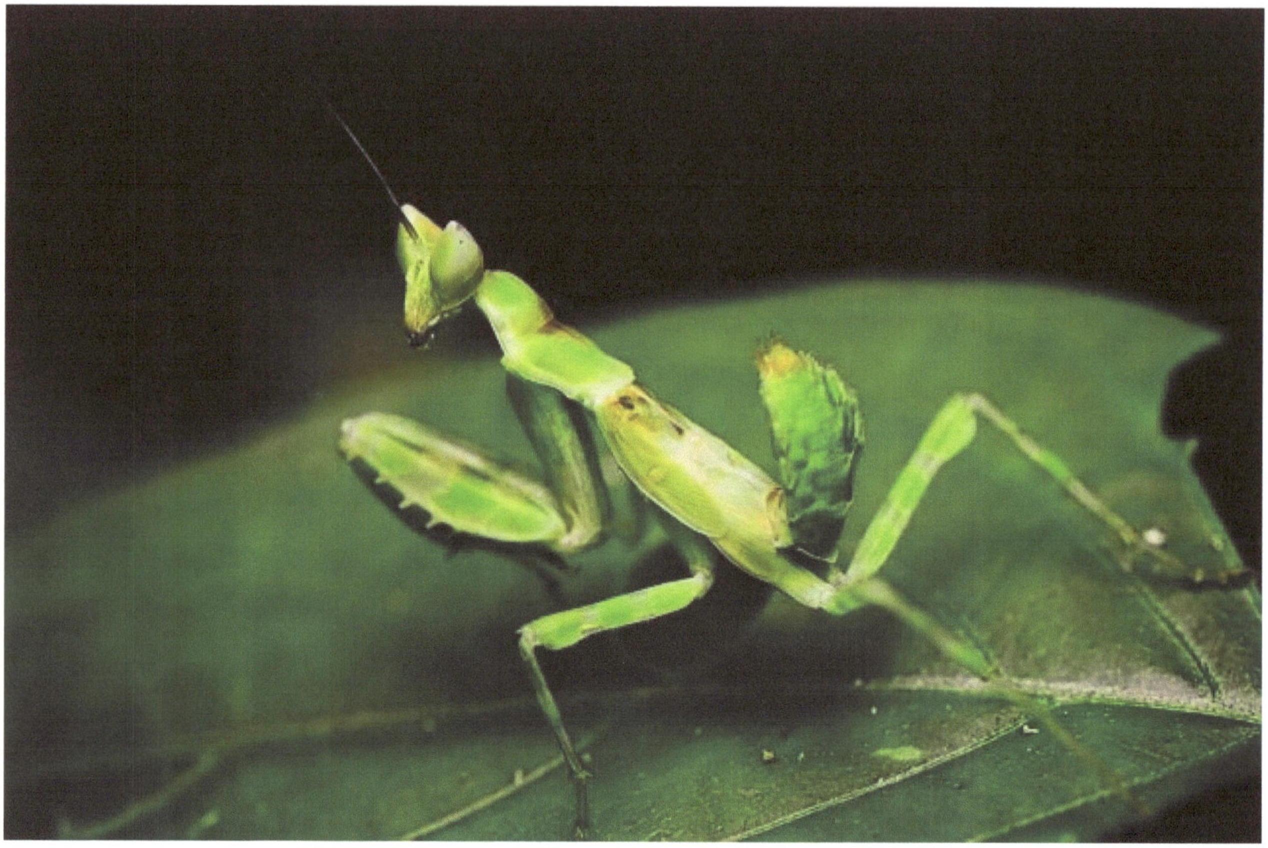

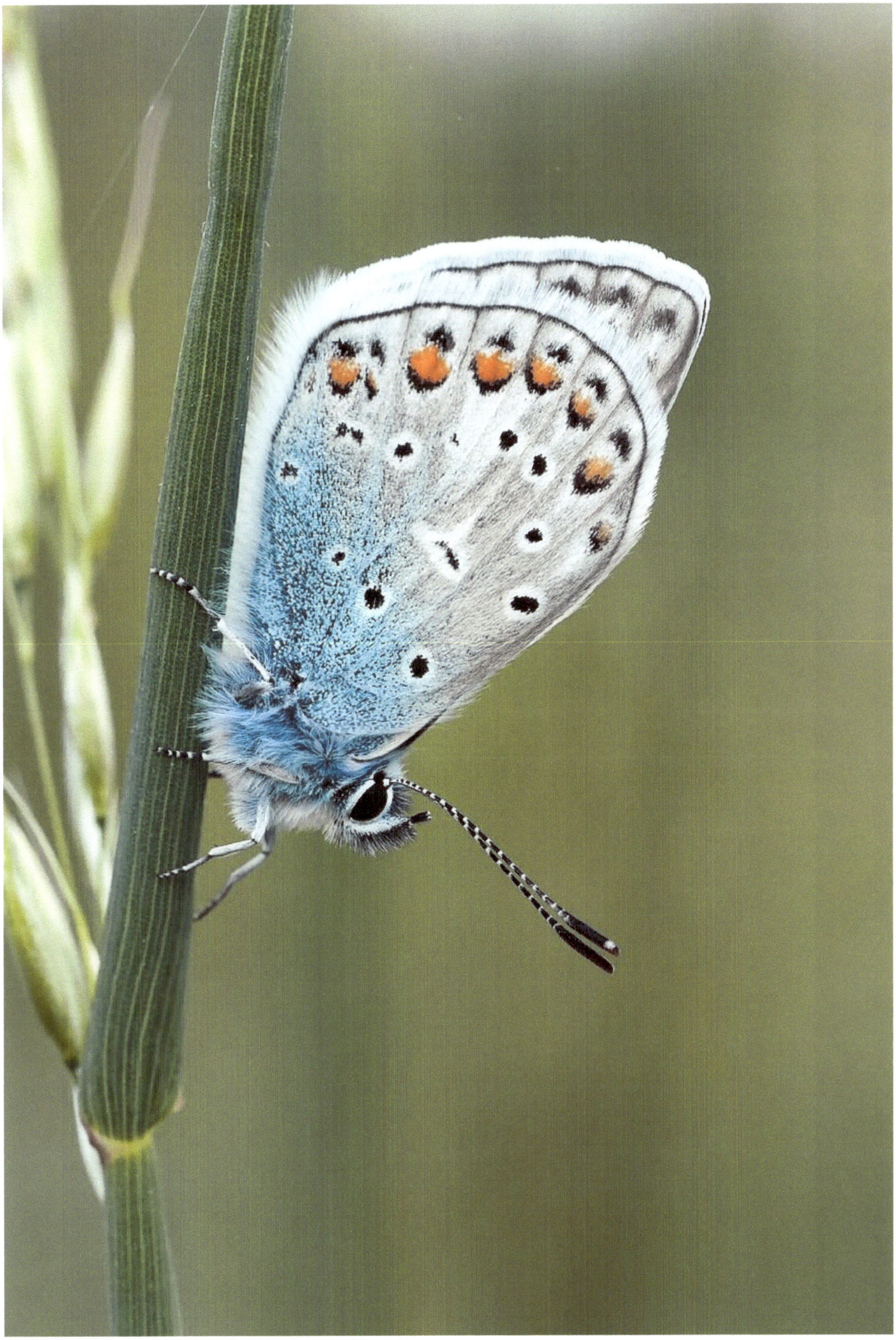

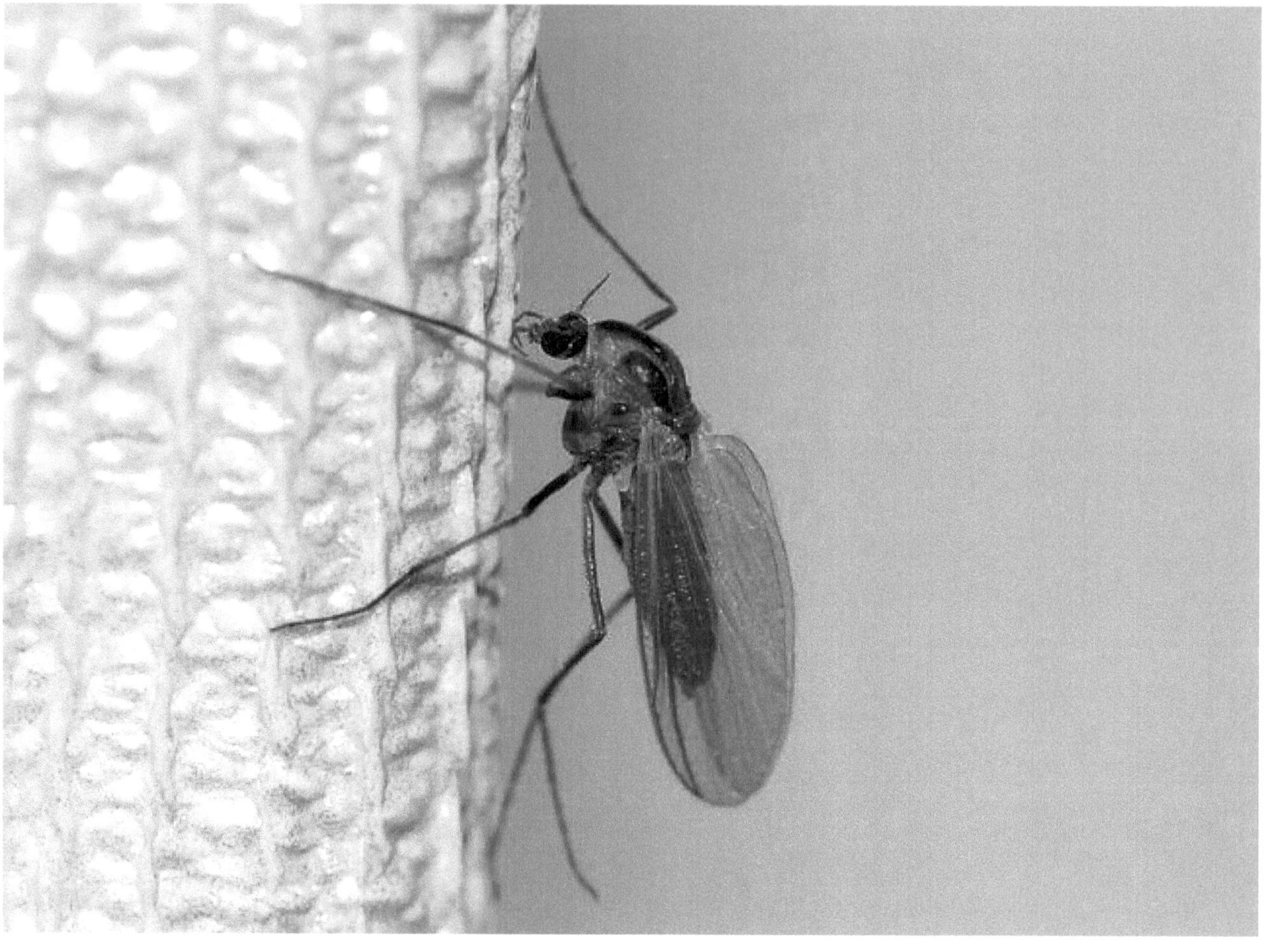

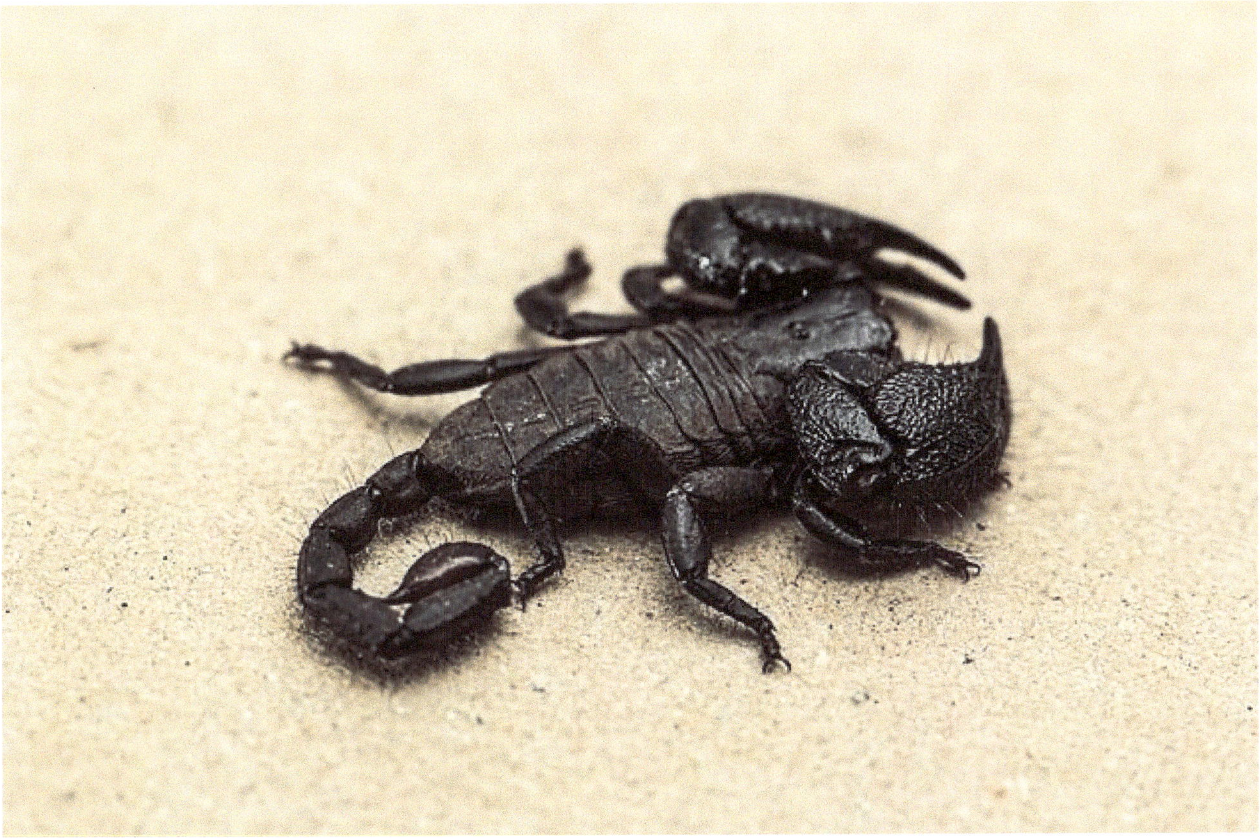

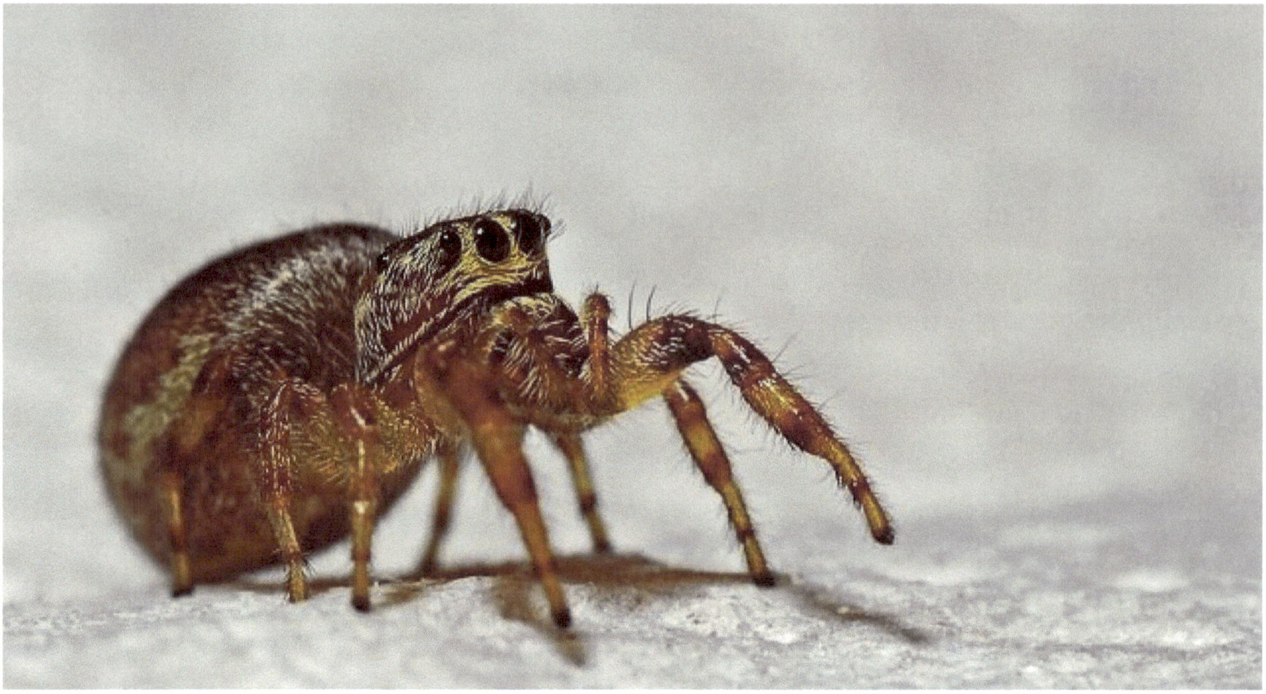

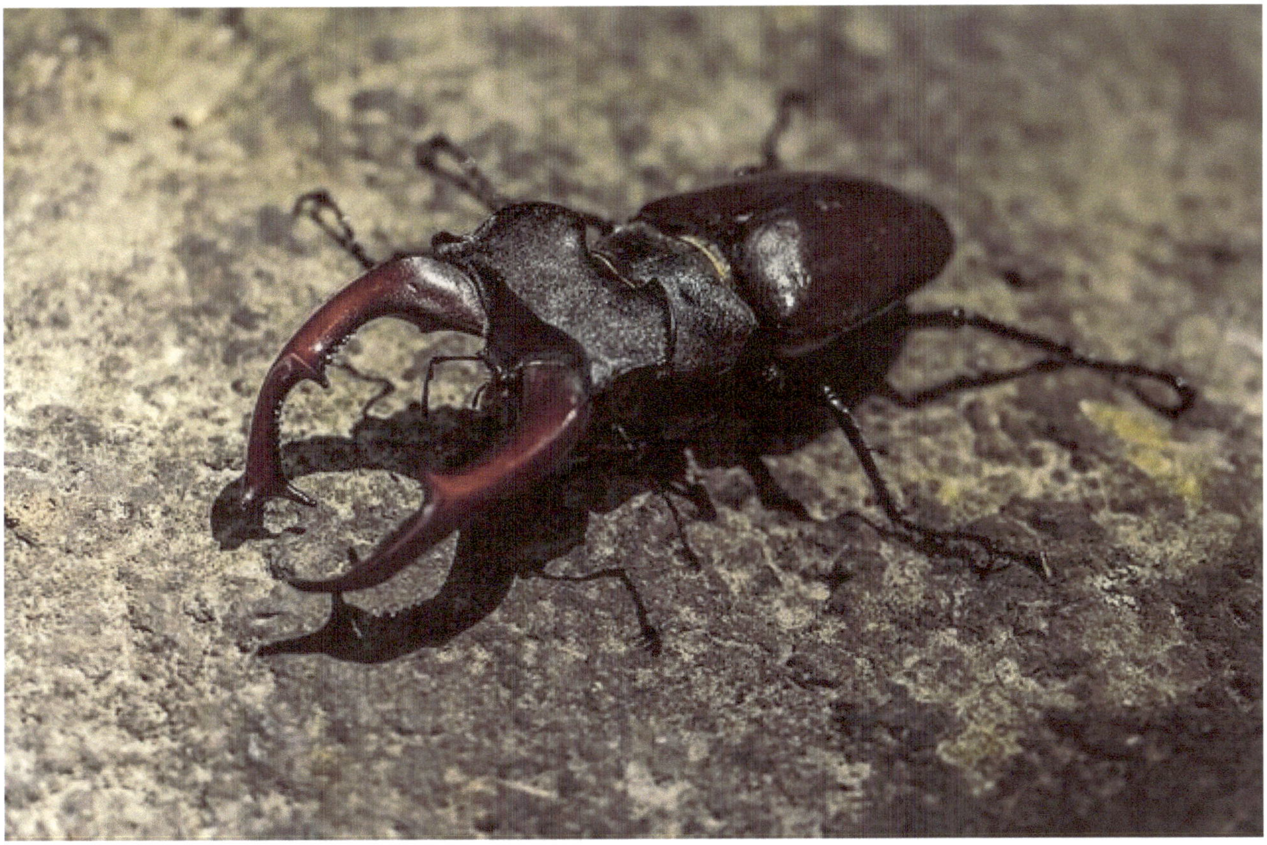

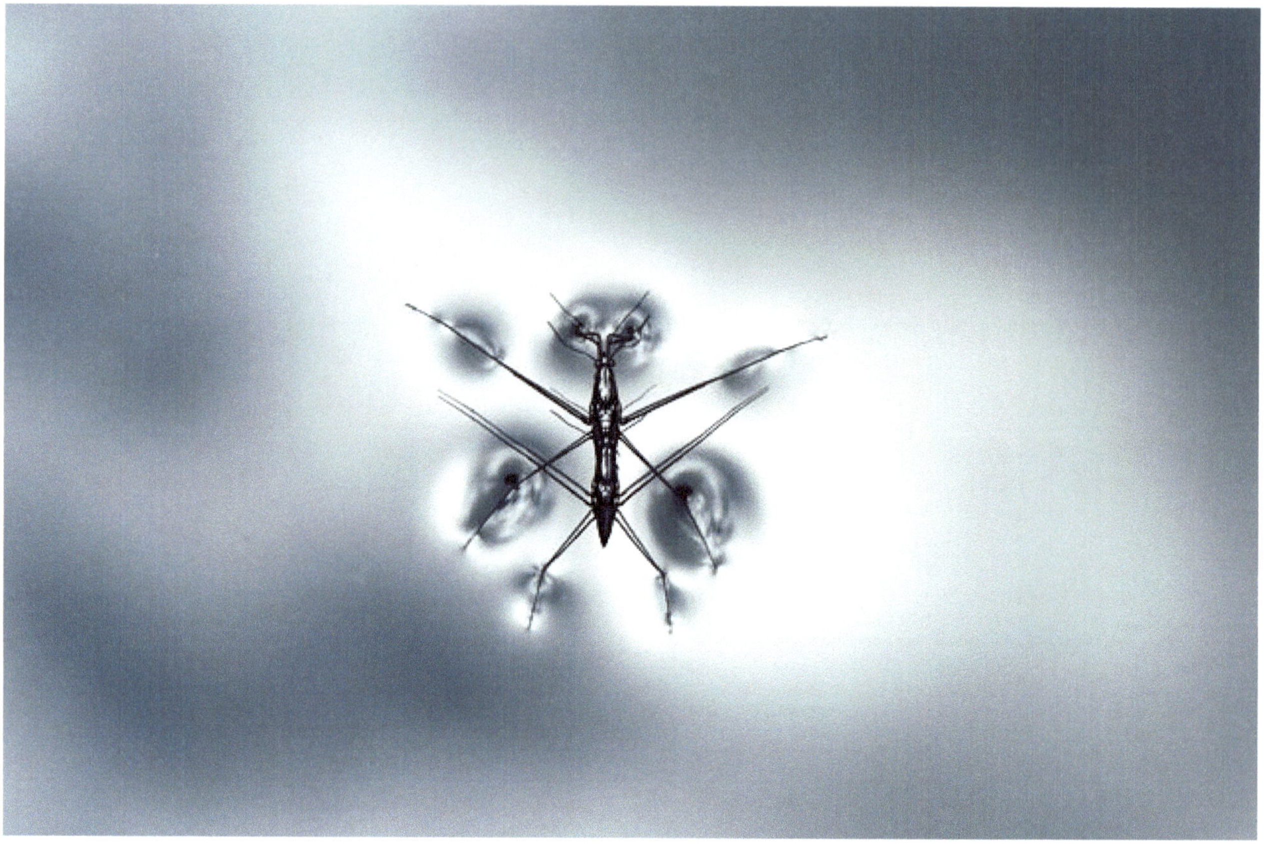

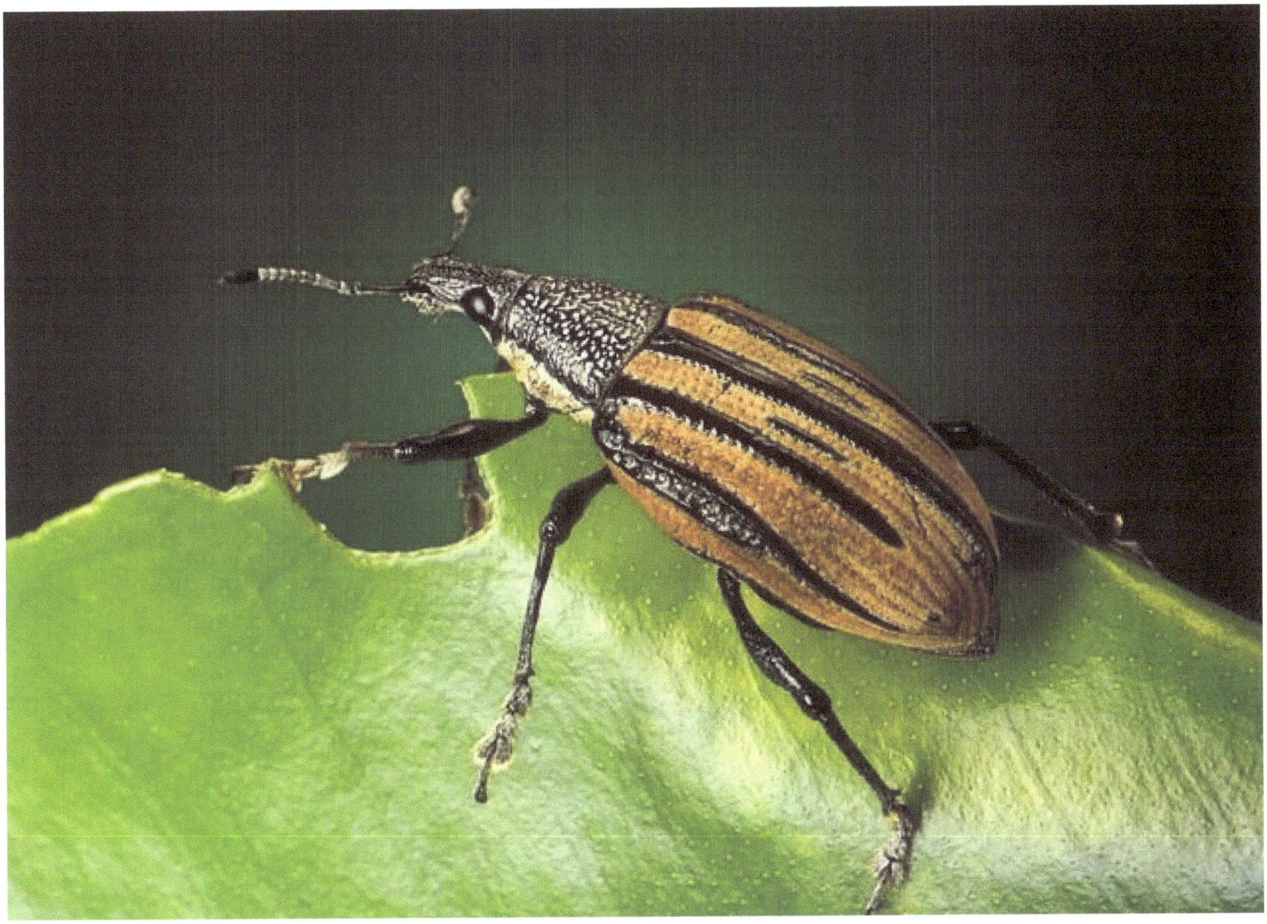

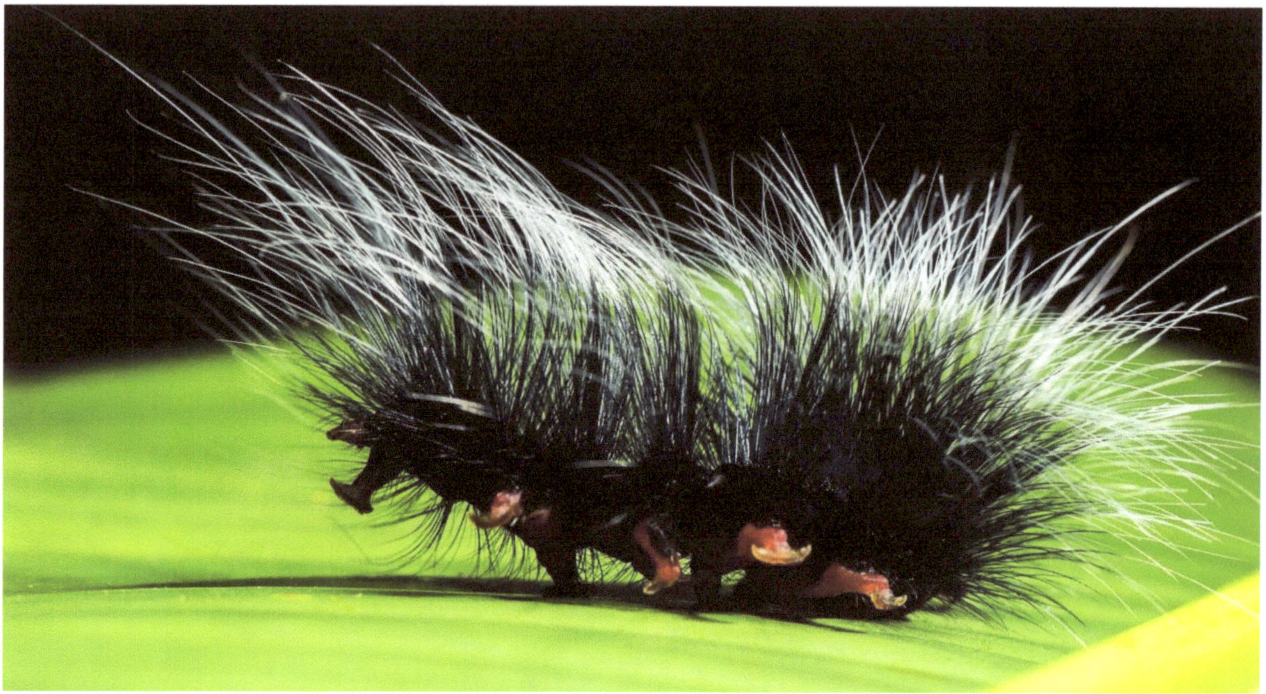

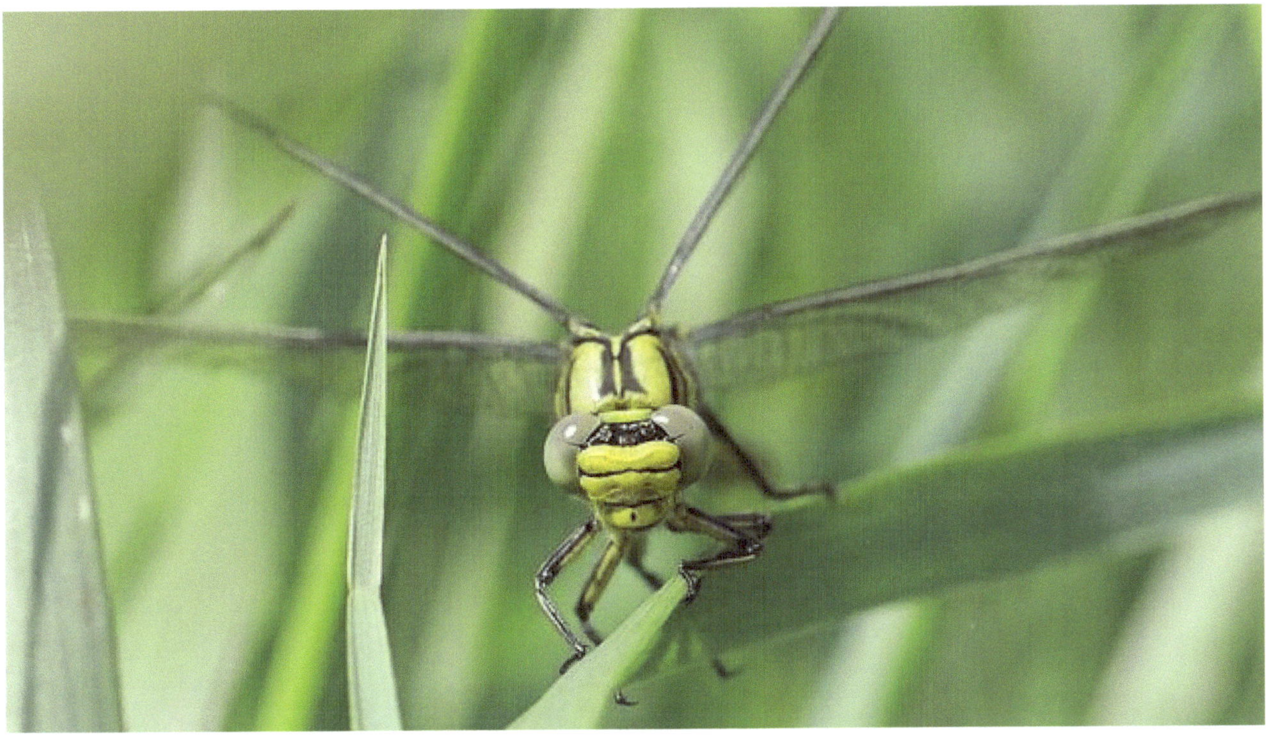

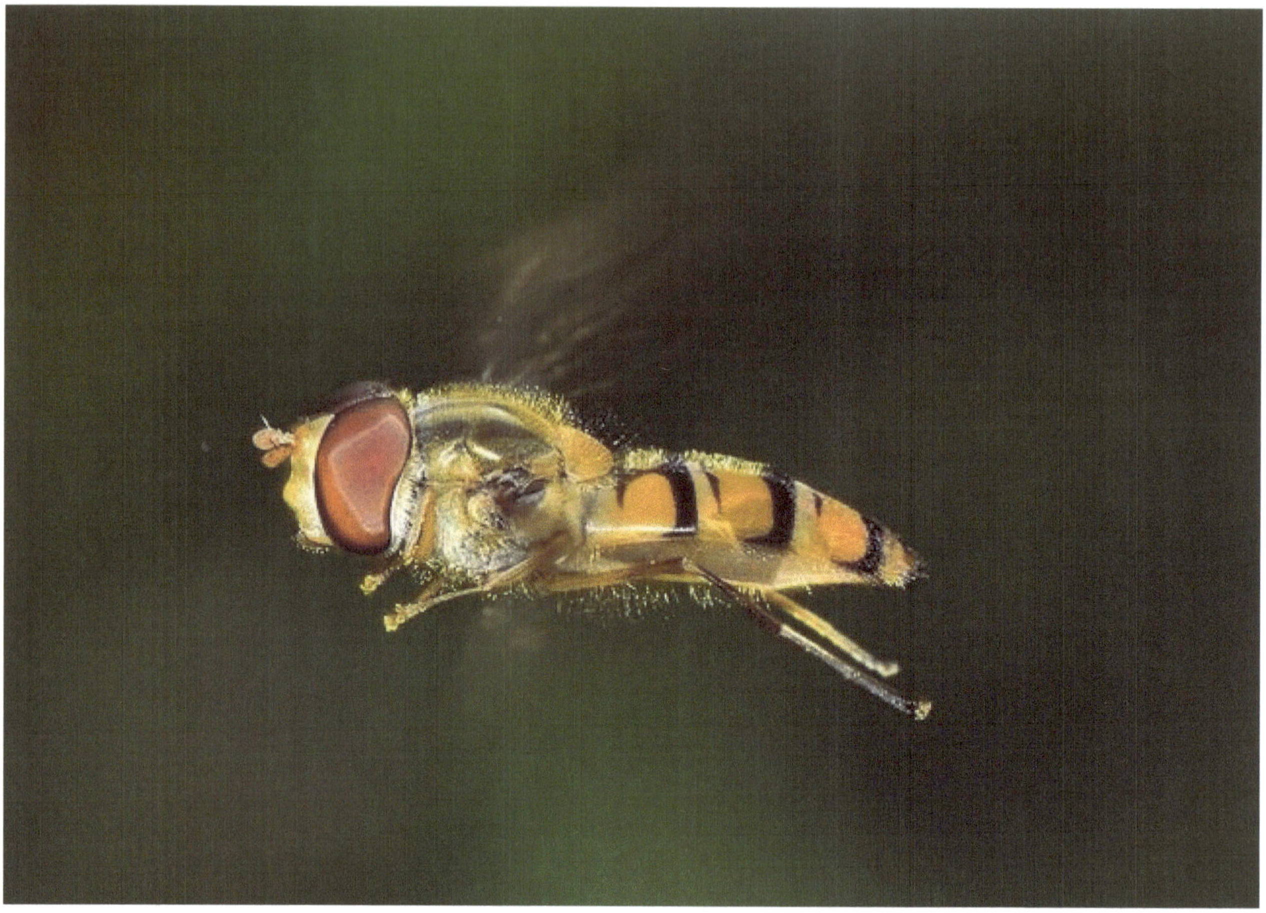

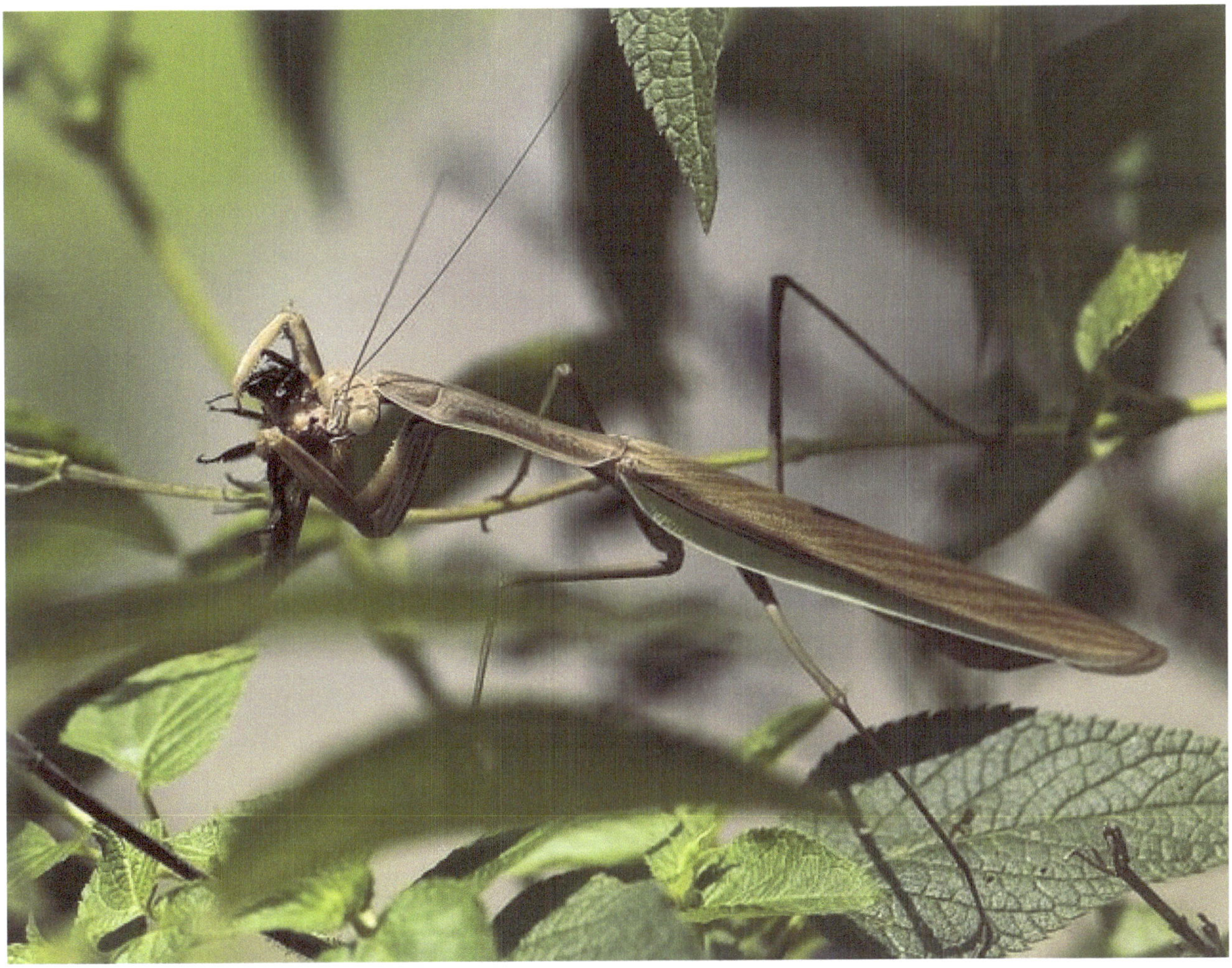

www.ingramcontent.com/pod-product-compliance
Lightning Source LLC
Chambersburg PA
CBHW060832290526
45792CB00006BB/1896
* 9 7 8 1 5 4 6 6 9 9 4 6 0 *